FROM MISFIRES TO HIRES

[How You Can *Supercharge* Your Talent Acquisition Team]

KATIE AND JEFF HOFFMAN

Also called **rim·man**. a person who

recopyeditor (def 3

cop·y·right

[**kop**-ee-rahyt]

noun

1.
the exclusive right to
musical, or artistic w
uch right by law o
he author or c

Cover and interior layout by Jodi McPhee.

ISBN: 978-1-6470495-3-9

gocorneroffice.com

Printed in the U.S.A.

IS THIS BOOK FOR YOU?

Not sure your team can be supercharged? Here are some burning doubts that many have before they begin optimizing efficiency, elevating team value, and improving retention rates.

1. **WHAT IF OUR TEAM IS ALREADY STRETCHED THIN, WITH NO TIME TO READ A BOOK, TAKE ON ADDITIONAL INITIATIVES, OR IMPLEMENT NECESSARY CHANGES?**

RESPONSE: We understand where you're coming from—when your team is already stretched thin, finding time to read a book or implement new initiatives can feel overwhelming. And consider this: if nothing changes, in the next 3 months, 6 months or even a year, will your situation improve, or will the same challenges continue to hold you back? This book is designed for exactly that scenario. It focuses on refining what you're already doing, with quick, high-impact strategies that streamline processes and eliminate redundancy. Transformational leaders lead and innovation is necessary to advance the mission of your department. If you're looking for a great starting point, this is it.

2. **WHAT IF WE ALREADY HAVE A TALENT ACQUISITION STRATEGY IN PLACE? I'M NOT SURE THIS BOOK CAN MAKE OUR HIRING PROCESS AND TALENT STRATEGIES BETTER?**

RESPONSE: This may be the case. While many organizations already have a talent acquisition strategy in place, even the best teams encounter challenges—as you will read about our team's challenges in the Introduction! This book goes beyond merely inundating you with more information—it's a blueprint for transformation! It's packed with foundational strategies, and coupled with our workbook full of actionable exercises, templates, and real-life examples, will empower you to make practical, meaningful changes. Designed to boost what you're already doing, it offers fresh approaches that fit the fast-changing recruitment landscape, so your team can stay ahead and keep improving.

3. OUR CHALLENGES ARE UNIQUE AND HOW DO I KNOW YOUR BOOK CAN DIRECTLY ADDRESS THEM? I AM SKEPTICAL ABOUT THE RETURN ON INVESTMENT.

RESPONSE: It is completely understandable how you may feel this way. It has been our experience that every company faces their own unique challenges, but the basics of successful talent acquisition are pretty universal. This book provides adaptable frameworks, templates, and strategies to tackle common issues, all of which you can tailor to fit your specific needs. You'll see a great return on investment through tangible improvements in key metrics like reduced time to hire, higher quality hires, and increased retention rates, all proven strategies that lead to measurable results for your organization!

4. THE PRICE OF THIS BOOK SEEMS A BIT HIGH. CAN'T I FIND SIMILAR CONTENT ONLINE FOR FREE?

RESPONSE: There is information online and if one has the time they can absolutely search, study, test, and potentially apply it, all of which requires time and commitment. *From Misfires to Hires* has already done the legwork, with more than a combined 75 years of hands-on recruiting, we have been able to sort out the processes and systems that work best. This book really simplifies years of proven experience and data-driven insights into a straightforward, step-by-step guide tailored for CHROs and Talent Acquisition leaders. It cuts through the noise and focuses on what really works. As for the price, think of it as an investment. The cost of a bad hire or an inefficient hiring process far outweighs the price of this book. With the practical strategies and templates inside, you'll boost your hiring success, reduce turnover, and save your company in the long run.

STOP. DON'T FORGET YOUR BONUS!

To ensure that you and your team get the most benefit possible from this book, we also want to share something with you that we usually reserve for our one-on-one clients. It's the **CornerOffice Leadership Competency Blueprint.**

Are you ready to transform your talent management strategy and unlock leadership potential across your organization?

Introducing the **CornerOffice Leadership Competency Blueprint,** a strategic tool designed for talent acquisition leaders, HR executives, recruiters, and CHROs to build and measure talent development strategies that drive success.

Here's why you need it:

KEY BENEFITS OF THE BLUEPRINT

1. LEADERSHIP CULTIVATION

Our blueprint provides a clear roadmap to enhance leadership qualities at all levels. Empower your leaders with the skills they need to meet today's challenges and navigate the future with confidence.

2. COMPREHENSIVE TALENT STRATEGY

The blueprint outlines essential competencies that serve as the cornerstone of all talent management processes—from recruitment and onboarding to professional development. With this tool, your talent strategy will align seamlessly with your company's overarching goals and values.

3. OBJECTIVE PERFORMANCE METRICS

Assess individual and team performance with clear, measurable metrics that ensure fair evaluations. This process helps you pinpoint areas for improvement while recognizing outstanding achievements.

4. CAREER DEVELOPMENT PATHWAYS

Equip employees with the insights they need to advance their careers. By clarifying necessary competencies, the blueprint helps your team focus on building the skills that matter most for their progression.

5. EFFECTIVE SUCCESSION PLANNING

Prepare for the future by identifying and developing the next generation of leaders. With this blueprint, your organization stays resilient and prepared for smooth leadership transitions, ensuring long-term continuity and growth.

6. STRATEGIC ALIGNMENT

Align individual competencies with your organization's strategic objectives. This not only drives better strategy execution but also fosters a high-performance culture that's built for success.

7. GLOBAL AND CULTURAL RELEVANCE

Designed with a global perspective, the blueprint ensures consistent leadership and competency standards across all geographic locations. This consistency fosters a unified corporate culture, no matter where your teams are based.

WHY IT MATTERS

The CornerOffice Leadership Competency Blueprint is more than just guidelines—it's a comprehensive tool to help you develop and harness talent across your organization. If you're aiming to build a resilient, adaptable, and strategically focused workforce ready to meet the demands of an ever-changing business landscape, this blueprint is essential.

Ready to take the next step? This **bonus** is here to help you do just that.

Receive the blueprint for you and your team at:
gocorneroffice.com/leadership-blueprint

WHAT READERS ARE SAYING ABOUT
FROM MISFIRES TO HIRES

"If you're tired of theory and ready for real change, these books are for you. *From Misfires to Hires* gets right to the heart of what we need—clear steps, smart strategies, and a path to better hires and higher retention."

—Drew McGlinchey, Sonepar USA,
Regional Vice President of Human Resources

"*From Misfires to Hires* is like having a secret tool for your talent acquisition strategy. The insights shared by CornerOffice showcases their deep expertise, strategic approach, and commitment to excellence make them an invaluable ally in finding and retaining top talent. With CornerOffice, you're not just filling roles—you're building a stronger, more resilient organization."

—Jerell Ringer, Principal Team Lead of a Quick Serve
Industry Leader, Staff Selection and Entity Operations

"CornerOffice has been pivotal in my career—first placing me at Chick-fil-A and later partnering with me at The Home Depot. Their understanding of both sides of talent acquisition is unparalleled. *From Misfires to Hires* captures the same expertise and actionable strategies that drive real hiring success. It's essential reading for any talent leader."

—Angela Holcomb, Fortune 20 Home Improvement Company,
Sr. Executive Recruiter

"These books are an inspirational resource for any talent leader looking to level up. The insights in *From Misfires to Hires* are like having a mentor by your side, guiding you to build a recruiting function that's sharp, strategic, and highly respected."

—Cynthia Cartmell Burns, Burns Lane Consulting,
President and Former CHRO Ingevity

"*From Misfires to Hires* effortlessly marries strategic insight with practical execution, a balance that is always a challenge for Talent leaders. If you're looking for tested and proven guidance that your teams can immediately implement to get ahead, this book is what you need!"

—Meghan Dougherty, Energy Industry Leader,
Vice President Talent and Organizational Development

"CornerOffice has been a trusted partner in every stage of my career—first placing me at Crawford Electric, then helping me build out our powerhouse teams. Their deep understanding of both the candidate and client sides is unmatched. *From Misfires to Hires* brings their expertise to life and is a must-have guide for any talent leader looking to elevate their hiring strategy."

—Megan Bishop, Crawford Electric,
Vice President Human Resources

CONTENTS

gocorneroffice.com

PREFACE

n today's competitive market, talent acquisition isn't just a function—it's the foundation of growth. Every company's success hinges on its ability to attract and retain the right people. But what's often overlooked is the one thing that can make or break your entire talent strategy: communication.

At **CornerOffice**, we've built our entire system around the belief that clear, intentional communication is the linchpin that holds together every stage of the recruitment process. From engaging top talent to creating alignment between hiring managers and HR leaders, communication drives results. It's how we've consistently achieved an impressive 91%+ retention rate for the candidates we place, ensuring long-term success for both the talent and the organizations we serve. By focusing on communication and alignment at every step, we've partnered with market-leading companies, to include prominent Fortune 100, across industries—helping them elevate their talent acquisition outcomes and achieve sustainable, long-term retention.

This book is designed to help you elevate and transform your talent acquisition process by leveraging communication as a strategic asset. We'll share the systems and processes that have consistently delivered long-term success for our partners, helping you to not only attract the right talent but retain them and foster their growth within your organization.

Whether you're a Chief Human Resources Officer (CHRO), Talent Acquisition Leader, HR professional, or even a business owner, our aim is to equip you with the tools you need to seamlessly implement our established strategies, systems and processes in your own organizations with the goal of elevating your recruitment outcomes.

We understand that as a busy leader, time is one of your most valuable resources. That's why this book is structured in an easy-to-navigate format, with actionable insights laid out clearly to save you time and effort. You'll be able to quickly pinpoint the strategies and processes that will have the most immediate impact, allowing you to

"We've been a trusted partner for market-leading Fortune 100 companies and global leaders across a variety of industries. Over the past decade, we've achieved a 91%+ retention rate within the first two years of employment for our clients, consistently exceeding expectations and driving long-term results."

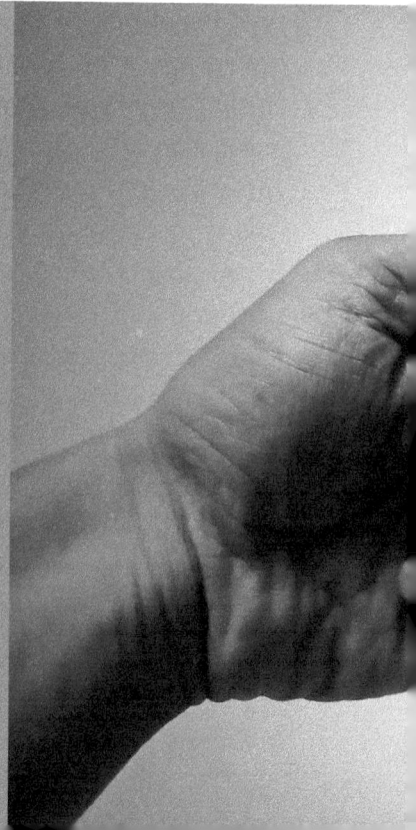

implement changes without feeling overwhelmed. We've crafted this guide to be a practical, effective resource that fits seamlessly into your already packed schedule.

Together, these elements form the foundation of the *From Misfires to Hires* series. Book 1—*How You Can Supercharge Your Talent Acquisition Team*—will guide you through the strategies, and Book 2—*The Ultimate Talent Acquisition Toolkit*—offers the elements of an interactive workbook with hands-on exercises, templates, and guides to put these strategies into action. We're excited to share this journey with you and help you achieve the results you've always aimed for.

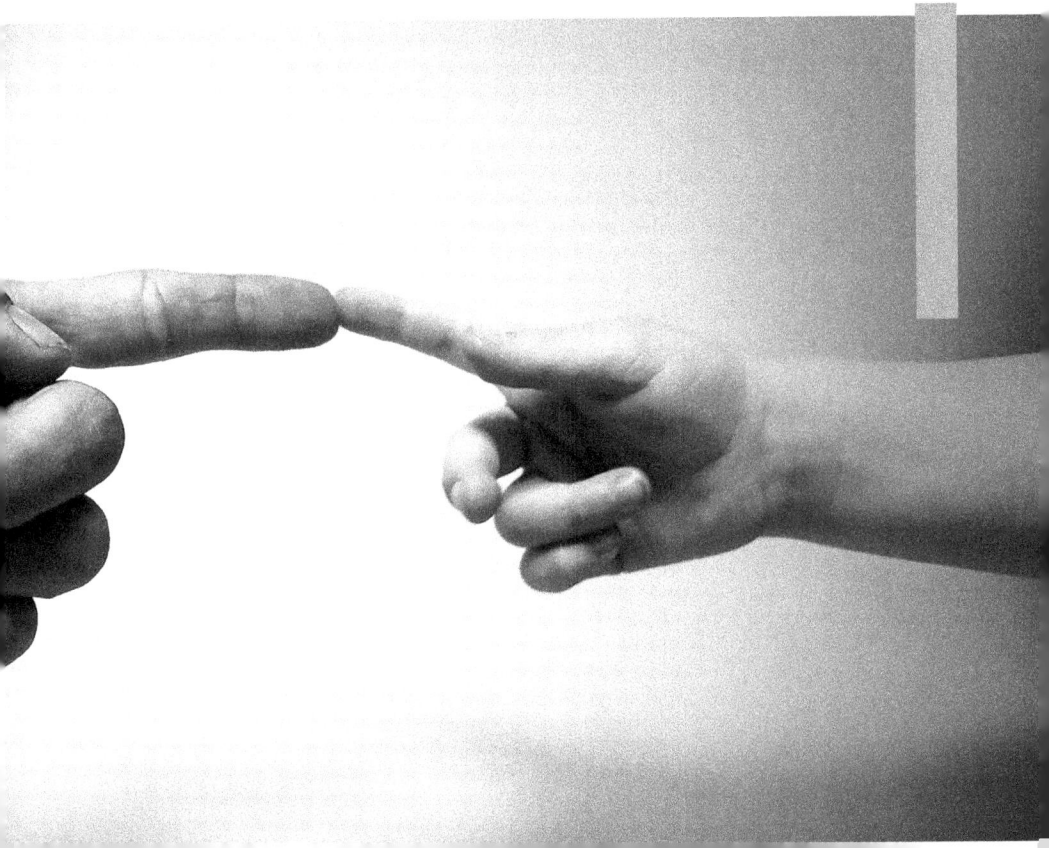

gocorneroffice.com

INTRODUCTION

A HUMBLE BEGINNING

When we first launched **CornerOffice** in 2014, we believed deep down that we had the expertise, drive, and vision to make a difference in executive recruitment. Yet, fear often crept in, weighing on our confidence. Like any boutique company competing against industry giants, we frequently questioned how we could stand out and whether our insights were innovative enough to truly impact leading experts in the field. As a family-owned boutique small business run by a husband and wife, we felt the pressure even more keenly, knowing that we had invested everything in a single venture. With so much competition, we often wondered if our approach was distinctive and if we could transform our commitment to personalized service and long-term success into meaningful, lasting partnerships with major clients.

The challenge we faced wasn't a lack of passion; we loved what we were doing and thrived on helping our partners. Instead, it was about overcoming the fears of self-doubt and nurturing our belief in our abilities. We needed to prove to ourselves that our skills could genuinely benefit our partners and that we could compete at the highest level. We began to experience small successes and received validation from partners who were excited about our services and sought our assistance. This bolstered our confidence and confirmed the demand for what we offered, reinforcing our belief in ourselves. We recognized that we possessed the necessary skills, and it was time to instill that same confidence in our clients.

LEARNING FROM THE PROCESS

In the early days, calls with companies like Chick-fil-A brought excitement but also pressure. Were we really ready for this? That pressure drove us to refine how we presented our value. We learned to ask better questions, listen more deeply, and earn our clients' trust through results.

A pivotal moment arose when our work with a Fortune 50 company led Katie to be considered for an internal role as part of their executive succession plan. It became evident that we were recognized not merely as another vendor, but as trusted and valued partners. Simultaneously, Jeff came across "Building a StoryBrand" by Donald Miller, which proved instrumental in refining our message and enhancing our communication of value. These moments of clarity not only contributed to our most successful year yet but also solidified our reputation as an industry leader.

THE ROAD TO SUCCESS

From that point, **CornerOffice** began to grow rapidly. We've been a trusted partner for market-leading Fortune 100 companies and global leaders across a variety of industries. Over the past decade, we've achieved a 91%+ retention rate within the first two years of employment for our clients, consistently exceeding expectations and driving long-term results.

This journey taught us that humility is a strength. We grew into our roles as leaders by staying true to our values, learning from each challenge, and refining our approach. Our journey to perfecting our systems and processes began even prior to the creation of **CornerOffice**, during our time in various recruiting industries. It was only when we ventured out on our own that we gained the freedom and autonomy to take risks, learn from failures, and build an effective **CornerOffice** way—driving the results that talent acquisition teams aspire to have. After over a decade of development, our approach is now ready for rapid implementation, yielding results in thirty days or less—transforming ten years of effort into immediate outcomes.

Now, we're excited to share those lessons with you so you can leap past the hard parts and find the same success—in way less time!

BUILDING THE BRIDGE BETWEEN STRATEGY AND ACTION

As you've learned from our journey, the road to building a successful talent acquisition strategy isn't just about filling positions—it's about creating a seamless process that aligns with your company's long-term vision. And the key to making that happen? Effective communication.

In this first book of the *From Misfires to Hires* series, we've laid the groundwork for you to supercharge your talent acquisition team. You'll find a comprehensive approach to leveraging communication to strengthen every aspect of the recruitment process—from finding right-fit candidates to ensuring long-term retention. But the journey doesn't stop here.

To truly bring these strategies to life, we've developed a companion book—*From Misfires to Hires: The Ultimate Talent Acquisition Toolkit*. This second book is designed to be your hands-on guide, filled with exercises, guides, and templates that help you implement everything you've learned here. While you can gain immense value from reading book 1 on its own, book 2 will help you put those strategies into action in real-time, turning theory into practice.

Whether you choose to continue with the full toolkit or begin with the strategic foundation laid out here, know that both resources are designed to give you the insights, processes, and practical tools to elevate your talent acquisition strategy and lead your team to long-term success.

> # PEOPLE ARE NOT YOUR MOST IMPORTANT ASSET. THE RIGHT PEOPLE ARE.
>
> *—JIM COLLINS*

Are you ready to enhance your ability to attract, hire, and retain the right people—those who align with your company's culture and values? Then turn the page, and let's get started in supercharging your company's talent acquisition together.

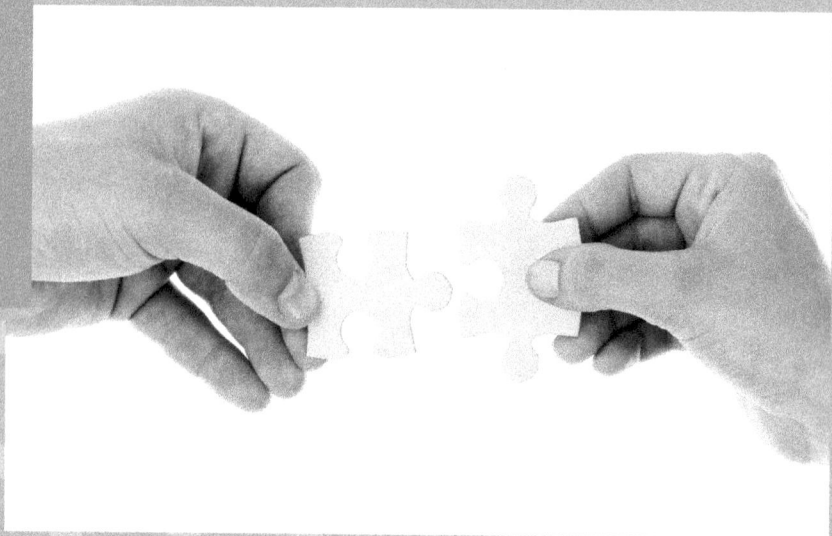

gocorneroffice.com

CHAPTER 1

NAVIGATING COMMUNICATION BREAKDOWNS: TACTICS FOR RESOLVING EFFECTIVELY

THE COMMUNICATION BREAKDOWN

Communication gaps frequently lead to missed opportunities, misunderstandings of job requirements and qualifications needed, and potential hires slipping away. Let's imagine a situation where a hiring manager does not clearly define the ideal qualifications for the role or the right candidate background to seamlessly fit into the team or when a recruiter neglects to clearly define the search guidelines to a hiring manager; all leading to conflicting expectations, a lengthy hiring journey, and a poor candidate experience.

After two decades of conversations with industry experts, talent leaders, and candidates, it has been repeatedly shown that recurring issues such as vague job descriptions and irregular feedback loops severely impede recruitment; emphasizing the concrete consequences of ineffective communication, and showing how promising candidates can easily fall through the cracks. In addition, continuing to have delays in filling open roles jeopardizes the company's success as there are several costs associated with gaps in talent.

BUILDING A ROBUST COMMUNICATION FRAMEWORK

To circumvent these potential issues, it is crucial to establish a well-defined and efficient communication framework. This process begins by crafting thorough job descriptions with hiring managers to make sure things are clear and on point. Equally important is setting up a system for ongoing feedback. This system needs to be quick and well-organized, making it a key part of the hiring process. For example, by having weekly check-ins and using standard feedback forms, we can improve communication and make the hiring process more efficient.

ORGANIZATIONAL CULTURAL IMPACT

Organizational culture has a huge impact on how we communicate. When a company values openness, transparency, and feedback, it naturally leads to better communication during recruitment. HR leaders play a key role in aligning recruitment communication with the company culture by promoting these values. This not only improves internal communication but also boosts employer branding and the employee experience, attracting candidates who fit the company culture.

LEVERAGING TECHNOLOGY IN COMMUNICATION

In the current digital era, technology plays a crucial role in enhancing communication. Solutions such as Applicant Tracking Systems (ATS) and Candidate Relationship Management (CRM) systems can automate and document interactions, guaranteeing no information is overlooked and maintaining consistent communication throughout the hiring stages. Despite the notable benefits these tools provide, they also present challenges. The impersonal aspect of automated messages may discourage candidate involvement, underscoring the importance of establishing a well-rounded strategy that integrates technology with continual personalized interactions.

ACTION STEPS

HOW TO APPLY THE INSIGHTS FROM THIS CHAPTER

- Create a workplace where communication thrives in talent acquisition, consider regularly updating communication methods to match the team's and candidates' changing needs.

- Communicate with candidates in a way that shows respect, transparency, and keeps them informed regardless of the outcome.

- Use technology wisely to improve, not replace, human interactions, making sure automation supports rather than hinders recruitment.

KEY TAKEAWAY

Effective communication in talent acquisition goes beyond sharing information. It's about building relationships and creating an environment that values clarity and openness. Constructive communication is essential in business. Organizations that excel in fostering open and honest dialogue between leaders and employees are positioned to gain the most advantages. Transparent and efficient communication helps to reduce conflicts, enhance employee engagement, boost productivity, cultivate a positive workplace culture, increase employee satisfaction, and drive innovation. As we move forward, we'll explore the ins and outs of recruiting and how a better communication plan can simplify and enhance these challenges, setting the stage for deeper talks on strategic talent management.

COMMUNICATION FLOWCHART

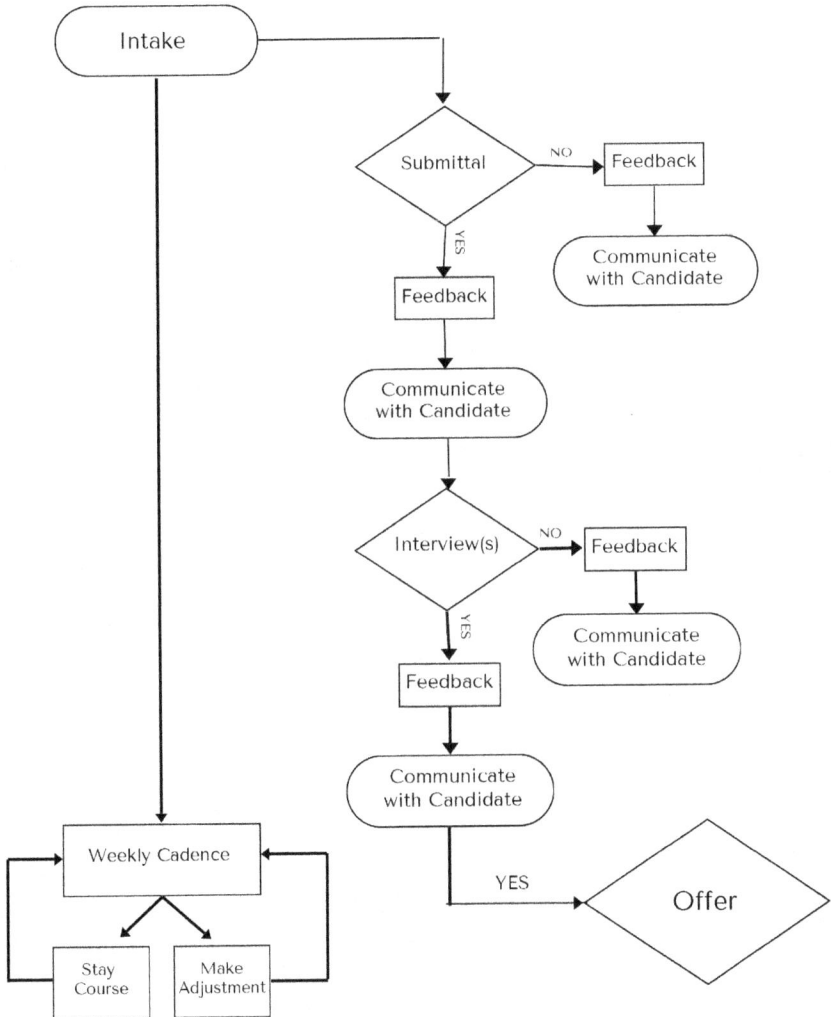

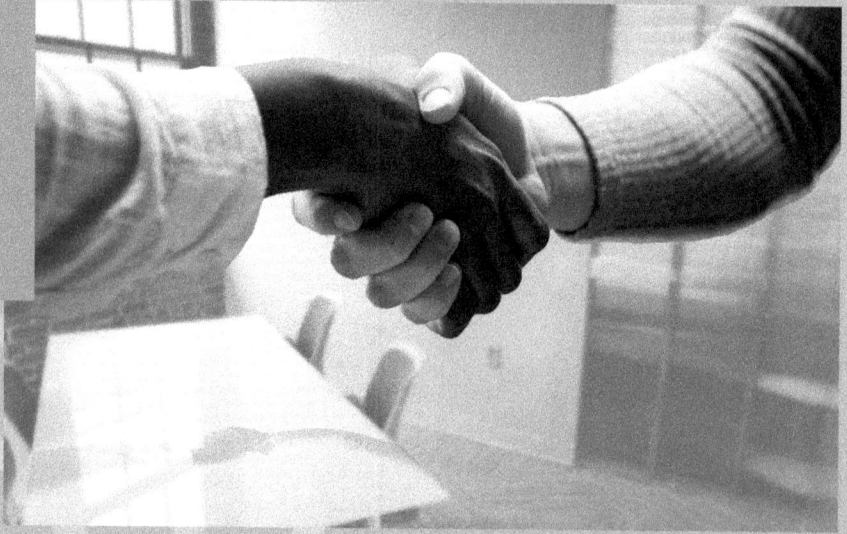
gocorneroffice.com

CHAPTER 2

UNMASKING THE HIRING MIRAGE: NAVIGATING THE COMPLEXITIES BEHIND THE CURTAIN

On the surface, the process of hiring may appear simple—posting a job, interviewing candidates, and extending an offer. Yet, the truth is far more complex. This chapter delves deeper into the nuanced challenges of the hiring process, offering strategies to navigate them effectively and elevate your team's success. This ensures a smoother, more efficient hiring experience for all involved.

THE MISCONCEPTION OF SIMPLICITY IN HIRING

Many individuals view the recruitment process as a straightforward transaction, yet it encompasses a nuanced interplay of various components—comprehending job prerequisites, harmonizing candidate anticipations, and managing organizational intricacies. The misinterpretation of its simplicity may culminate in hasty verdicts and insufficient candidate evaluation; however if you learn and embrace the nuances and follow a more deliberate strategy you will have enormous success. Let's explore four real-life scenarios where these misunderstandings resulted in expensive recruitment blunders.

#1: CONFIDENTIAL NIGHTMARE

A hiring manager asked the talent partners to conduct a confidential search, which added some challenges to the hunt. Reluctantly, they agreed as they understood the reasons behind the confidentiality of the search. The hiring manager set the expectation that the team could not mention nor reveal the company to potential candidates, but also couldn't disclose the industry or state to avoid giving away the company's identity. Despite knowing this approach would be daunting and despite their advice to the hiring manager, the talent team put up a brave front and followed the directions. Fast forward a year, the position remained unfilled. Why? Well, the job requirements were very specific, the talent team struggled to get responses due to limited information, and good candidates backed out upon learning more about the company and location.

BE BOLD: The talent team should act as consultants, drawing on their expertise. If they had warned about these issues and proposed confidentiality agreements as a solution, they could have saved time and money.

#2: NOT ALIGNED

The talent team receives a new search assignment. They schedule an intake call with the hiring manager, have a productive discussion, and note down all the essential requirements for the ideal candidate. Based on the information gathered in the intake call, they dive into sourcing talent that matches the hiring manager's request, and arrange interviews with the relevant individuals. The team recommends some excellent candidates based on the search criteria. The hiring manager throws a curve and now wants to include the department head as an additional interviewer into the process. This new addition is not convinced that any of the candidates fit and rejects them all. It turns out the department head has a completely different perspective on the qualifications! Now, back to the starting line.

LESSON LEARNED: The talent team must ensure alignment among all members of the hiring team and department heads right from the start. This setback prolongs the search process, and leaving a position vacant consumes a significant amount of time and money.

#3: "I WILL KNOW THEM WHEN I SEE THEM"

This statement is something many hiring managers say. It usually goes like, "I'll know the right person when I meet them." This is a disastrous approach that will lead to confusion and a complete waste of time. It shows the manager struggles to articulate what they need, so the talent expert should step in and guide them through with some questions. As a talent recruiter, you're the hiring pro—use your expertise to advise the manager on best practices. Ask about the role, the skills needed, and the personality traits that fit the team and culture. Once you outline the ideal candidate, it'll click for the hiring manager!

BE THE EXPERT: Guide the manager, don't just throw random candidates their way. By painting a clear picture of the perfect candidate upfront, you save time and money for all involved.

#4: GATHERING THE DETAIL

It is crucial to ask the candidates about their compensation expectations from the very beginning and be sure it matches the hiring team's range. This helps set expectations and not waste everyone's time. After weeks of interviewing, an offer is extended to the favored candidate however the offer is lower than the candidate had clearly stated as the expectation and it is turned down. Ugh, starting over. This should never happen and it is important to guide the hiring team on making sure the offer is competitive and matches the candidate's expectations. The hiring team should have never interviewed them if they did not think they could meet that expectation. Finally another great candidate is presented and this candidate will now get an offer that works for everyone. It's accepted, hooray!

THE LESSON HERE: Gather the compensation expectations from the first touch point, better to know if this is the right fit than to waste everyone's time and end up with disappointment all around.

DECONSTRUCTING THE NUANCES OF THE HIRING PROCESS

Understanding the intricacies of the hiring process and establishing a robust groundwork for success.

- **JOB ANALYSIS AND DESCRIPTION ACCURACY**
  - The importance of conducting a comprehensive job analysis cannot be overstated as it is crucial to capture the true essence of the requirements and why the role needs to exist.
  - Strategies for creating accurate and engaging job descriptions that attract the right candidates.

- **EMBRACING INNOVATION IN RECRUITMENT**
  - The importance and benefits of innovation and why traditional recruitment methods are outdated and how innovation enhances candidate experience and employer branding.
  - Exploring creative sourcing methods like chatbots, niche job boards, podcasts, VR, and recruitment events to attract top talent.
  - Learn contemporary assessment techniques including skills tests, and AI-powered evaluations for fair and efficient hiring.

- **CANDIDATE SOURCING AND SCREENING**
  - Overview of sourcing strategies, including the use of digital platforms and networking.
  - Best practices for candidate screening to ensure a strong technical and cultural fit.
  - To better match suitable candidates with the manager's requirements, it is important to request and understand the assessment questions from each hiring manager.

- **REVAMPING YOUR INTERVIEW PROCESS: EMBRACING INNOVATIVE TECHNIQUES**
  - Understand why traditional interview methods need updating and the benefits of innovative techniques.
  - Explore new interview methods like asynchronous interviews (one-way interviews), video intros, and gamification to enhance candidate evaluation.

- **INTERVIEWING TECHNIQUES**
  - Discuss the art and science behind effective interviewing.
  - Introduce structured interview techniques in tackling biases and honing in on key candidate attributes that truly matter. Delve into how these methods revolutionize the hiring process, paving the way for fairer and more insightful assessments.

- **OVERCOMING COMMON CHALLENGES**
  - **Aligning Stakeholder Expectations:** Ensure that hiring managers, recruiters, and executives are on the same page.
  - **Handling Communication Gaps:** Maintain clear and consistent communication throughout the hiring process.
  - **Technological Integration:** Best practices for integrating technology without losing the personal touch is essential in candidate interactions.

- **STRATEGIC ENHANCEMENTS FOR EFFICIENCY**
  - ○ **Automating Routine Processes:** The utilization of technology plays a crucial role in automating administrative tasks, thereby freeing up valuable time for engaging in strategic decision-making processes.
  - ○ **Data-Driven Decision Making:** By harnessing the power of data analytics to enhance the hiring process from sourcing the right candidates to making that final selection.
  - ○ **Building a Talent Pipeline:** Long-term strategies for creating a reservoir of potential candidates, reducing time-to-hire for future positions.

[

"Many individuals view the recruitment process as a straightforward transaction, yet it encompasses a nuanced interplay of various components—comprehending job prerequisites, harmonizing candidate anticipations, and managing organizational intricacies."

]

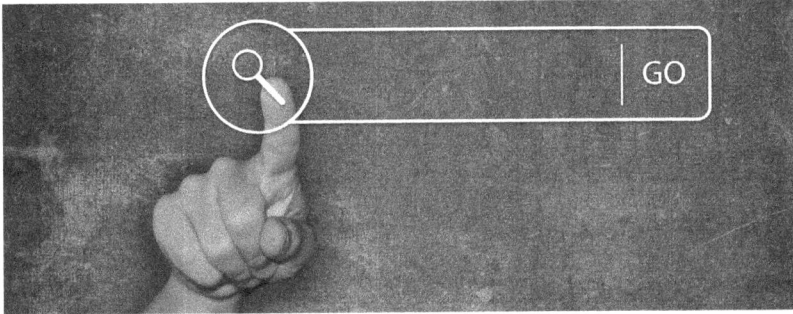

ACTION STEPS

HOW TO APPLY THE INSIGHTS FROM THIS CHAPTER

- Review and refine your job description process to ensure clarity and accuracy.

- Think about what new creative sourcing methods could work for your team.

- Implement at least one new interviewing technique discussed to enhance your selection process.

- Assess your current use of technology in hiring and identify one area for improvement.

KEY TAKEAWAY

When striving for successful hiring, it's important to understand that it involves a combination of implementing updated methods, clear communication, strategic planning, and careful execution. By delving into the intricacies highlighted in this chapter, businesses have the opportunity to elevate their hiring effectiveness and steer clear of the risks associated with oversimplifying the process. If you dig a little deeper and clearly communicate your strategies, directions and training with your talent and hiring teams, this new foundation will elevate your business's success.

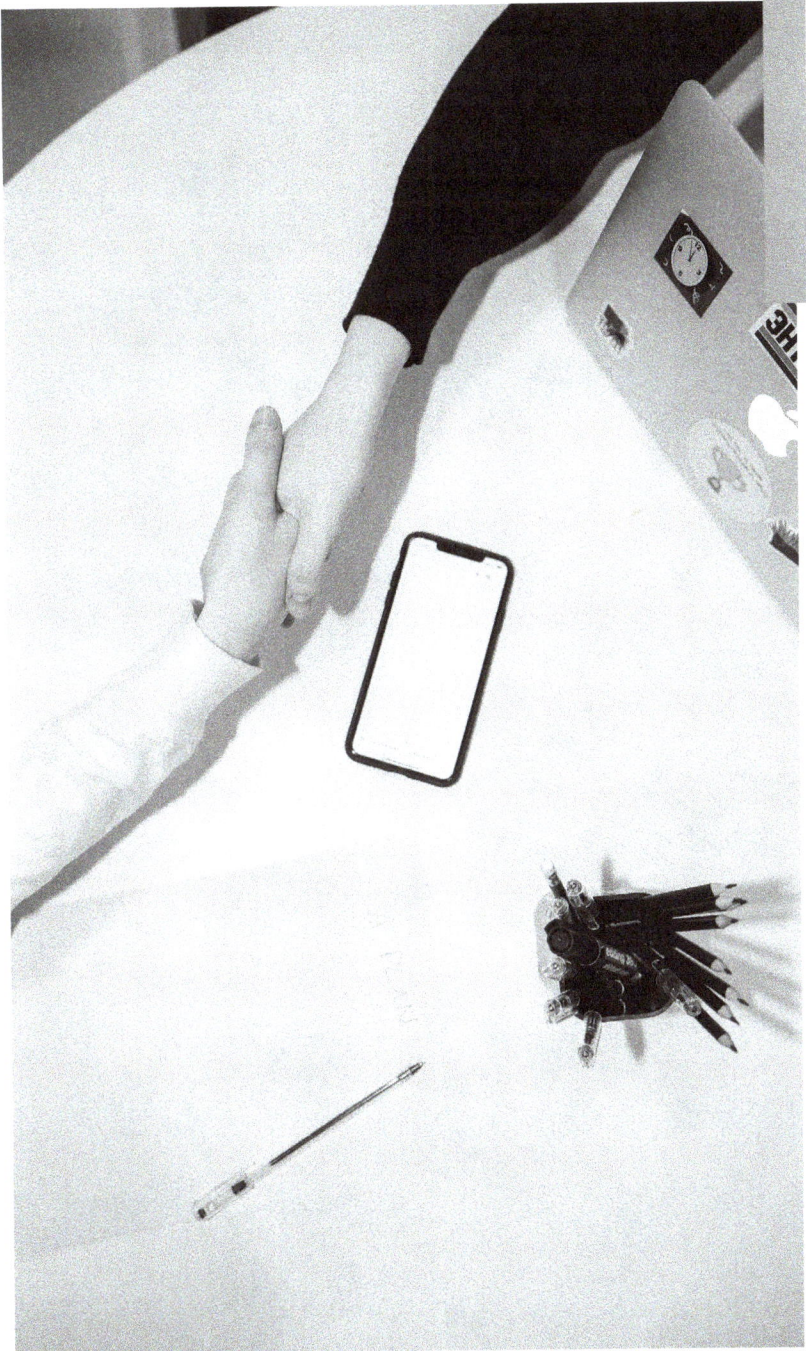

gocorneroffice.com

CHAPTER 3

JOB DETECTIVE: CRACKING THE CODE OF ROLE ANALYSIS AND DESCRIPTION

INTRODUCTION TO JOB ANALYSIS

Job analysis is a fundamental HR function that involves identifying and detailing the specific job duties and requirements, as well as the importance of these duties for a given job. The process is crucial in capturing the true essence of what a role entails and forms the foundation for many HR activities, including recruitment, performance management, and compensation. For new talent leaders, understanding how to conduct an effective job analysis is key to ensuring that all subsequent HR processes are aligned with actual job needs across various industries.

CONDUCTING EFFECTIVE JOB ANALYSIS

To perform a comprehensive job analysis, talent acquisition professionals should follow these structured steps:

- **INFORMATION GATHERING**
  - Collect data on job activities through various methods such

as observing incumbents, interviewing employees and supervisors, and reviewing job performance data. Engaging employees who currently hold the position provides insight into daily tasks and required skills that may not be captured through other means.

- **ANALYSIS TOOLS**
  - Utilize software and technologies designed for job analysis to organize and interpret the data collected. These tools can help in documenting repetitive tasks, necessary physical and mental skills, and the working environment of the job.

DEVELOPING ACCURATE AND ENGAGING JOB DESCRIPTIONS

Once you know what you need and who you want, it's time to attract your talent match. An accurate job description is a strategic tool in attracting the right candidates. It should include:

- **JOB TITLE AND SUMMARY**
  - Clearly state the job title and provide a brief summary that captures the essence of the role in a few sentences.

- **RESPONSIBILITIES**
  - List primary and regular tasks in order of importance.

- **QUALIFICATIONS**
  - Specify education, experience, skills, and certifications required.

- **BENEFITS AND COMPANY CULTURE**
  - Highlight unique benefits and aspects of company culture to

make the position attractive. Also include who will be working with this person, type of team and setting.

- **SALARY**
  - It is an excellent idea to include the salary or compensation package information. It shows transparency and helps not waste anyone's time.

STRATEGIES TO ENHANCE ACCURACY AND ENGAGEMENT

- **USE CLEAR, CONCISE, AND JARGON-FREE LANGUAGE THAT IS INCLUSIVE AND BROADLY UNDERSTANDABLE**

- **REGULARLY UPDATE THE JOB DESCRIPTIONS TO REFLECT ANY CHANGES IN THE ROLE OR COMPANY POLICIES**

CHALLENGES AND COMMON MISTAKES

Common pitfalls in job analysis and description writing include:

- **OVERSIMPLIFICATION**
  - Avoid glossing over complexities of the job which can lead to unmet expectations.
  - Job descriptions must evolve as the role or technology changes to avoid becoming outdated.

To address these challenges, conduct regular reviews and updates of job analysis and descriptions, and ensure that they are checked for relevance and accuracy by multiple stakeholders, this is an especially important step when posting a job, either a new hire or a backfill.

ACTION STEPS

HOW TO APPLY THE INSIGHTS FROM THIS CHAPTER

- **Worksheets and Templates**
  - ○ Provide templates for job analysis documentation and job description writing to standardize these processes across the organization.
  - ○ Include worksheets that prompt the user to ask the right questions during job analysis interviews and observations

- **Practical Exercises**
  - ○ Include exercises where learners can practice drafting job descriptions based on hypothetical job analysis data.
  - ○ Offer critique sessions where learners review and suggest improvements for real job descriptions.

KEY TAKEAWAY

Conducting thorough job analysis and crafting precise job descriptions is crucial for attracting and retaining the right talent. By gathering and analyzing job data, you can craft accurate, engaging job descriptions that attract the right candidates and set clear expectations. Regular updates and reviews help avoid common pitfalls and keep job descriptions relevant. Using templates and practical exercises will streamline the process, ensuring consistency and alignment with real job needs across your organization.

gocorneroffice.com

CHAPTER 4

RECRUITING REIMAGINED: ATTRACTING TOP TALENT WITH A TWIST

EMBRACING INNOVATION IN RECRUITMENT

In today's rapidly evolving job market, companies that embrace innovative recruitment strategies stand out from the competition. The process is straightforward, advertise/search, engage, screen and assess, however traditional methods no longer suffice; the key to attracting top talent lies in adopting creative and modern approaches. This chapter explores the process along with the essence of innovative recruitment, highlighting its benefits and offering practical tips for talent leaders to revolutionize their hiring processes.

Finding candidates for a role not only involves encouraging them to apply for a role based on a job advertisement but also involves proactively identifying potential hires for job openings. This proactive method is crucial in today's competitive job market, where the right talent can make a big difference in a company's success. For new talent leaders, mastering sourcing techniques is key to creating a strong talent pool and attracting qualified applicants consistently.

THE NEED FOR INNOVATION IN RECRUITMENT

The recruitment landscape has changed dramatically in recent years, driven by technological advancements and shifting candidate expectations. Job seekers today are more discerning and value a seamless, engaging hiring experience. A staggering 76% of candidates say a positive recruitment experience influences their decision to accept a job offer, while 52% have turned down offers due to a poor hiring process.

Innovative recruitment strategies not only enhance the candidate experience but also expand the talent pool and improve employer branding. Companies that fail to innovate risk losing out on top talent and falling behind in a competitive market.

BENEFITS OF INNOVATIVE RECRUITMENT

Understanding the intricacies of the hiring process and establishing a robust groundwork for success.

- **ATTRACTING TOP TALENT**
  - Elite candidates are drawn to companies known for treating applicants well. An innovative approach ensures a positive candidate experience, encouraging highly qualified individuals to spread the word.

- **WIDENING THE TALENT POOL**
  - Creative sourcing strategies reach candidates where they are, attracting passive candidates who aren't actively job hunting but could be a perfect fit.

- **BOOSTING EMPLOYER BRANDING**
  - ○ Candidates assess employer branding by considering factors like work-life balance, promotion prospects, and diversity, equity, and inclusion (DEI) policies. Innovative recruitment helps showcase a company's unique value proposition.

- **INCREASING EFFICIENCY**
  - ○ Innovation streamlines the recruitment process, from sourcing and job description writing to candidate assessments, interview scheduling, and onboarding.

EFFECTIVE CANDIDATE SOURCING STRATEGIES

To build a successful candidate sourcing strategy, talent acquisition professionals should employ a variety of methods that are widespread and common:

- **LEVERAGE MULTIPLE CHANNELS**
  - ○ Utilize job boards, social media platforms, professional networking sites, and employee referral programs to reach a broad audience.

- **TARGETED RECRUITMENT**
  - ○ Focus on niche platforms and professional groups that cater to specific industries or skill sets.

- **ENGAGE PASSIVE CANDIDATES**
  - ○ Develop strategies to attract candidates who are not actively looking for a job but might be interested in new opportunities.

INNOVATIVE SOURCING STRATEGIES

If you have engaged the basics and had no success, maybe it is time to give more innovative methods a try, or simply use them to enhance what the team is currently doing alongside the post and pray method.

- **GEO-FENCING**
  - One intriguing strategy involves drawing from marketing tactics and leveraging geofencing to boost job openings and enhance employment branding. This method effectively targets specific skill sets and is further beneficial as data informs targeting decisions.

- **CHATBOTS ON CAREER PAGES**
  - AI-powered chatbots can enhance the candidate experience by answering questions about job postings, providing additional information, and guiding applicants through the process. While effective, it's important to maintain human touchpoints to keep the experience organic and welcoming.

- **TEXT RECRUITING**
  - Text messaging offers a quick, personalized way to communicate with candidates, especially younger ones. However, it's crucial to ensure compliance and avoid spamming potential hires. Personalized texts can humanize the recruitment phase, but critical messages should be double-checked for accuracy.

- **COMPANY PODCASTS**
  - Podcasts featuring current employees discussing their roles and company culture provide candidates with an insider's view. This medium is particularly effective for early and

mid-career applicants, enhancing the employer brand and attracting passive candidates.

- **VIRTUAL REALITY (VR)**
  - Though still emerging, VR can offer immersive workplace tours and role previews, engaging candidates in a unique way. However, poorly executed VR experiences can be counterproductive, so quality is paramount.

- **NICHE JOB BOARDS**
  - Posting on specialized job platforms like those for accountants or developers can attract highly relevant candidates. This strategy ensures job ads reach the right audience, broadening the talent pool.

- **RECRUITMENT EVENTS**
  - Hosting in-person or hybrid recruitment events can significantly boost employer branding. These events provide an opportunity to connect with candidates directly, showcase company culture, and make a lasting impression.

- **SHOWCASING EMPLOYEE BENEFITS**
  - In a competitive job market, benefits beyond salary matter. Highlighting flexible work arrangements, health benefits, and development opportunities can make your company more attractive to potential hires.

- **EMPLOYEE REFERRAL PROGRAMS**
  - Encouraging current employees to refer candidates can be highly effective. Offering generous rewards for referrals, even if they don't lead to immediate hires, can motivate employees to participate actively.

- **ACCESSIBLE TALENT COMMUNITIES**
  - Building online talent communities allows you to engage with potential candidates continuously. Social media platforms can help manage these communities, providing a space for sharing job postings and company updates.

CANDIDATE SCREENING

Candidate screening is the process of evaluating sourced candidates to determine if they meet the requirements of the job. This step is crucial to narrowing down the applicant pool to those most likely to succeed in the role.

CONDUCTING EFFECTIVE CANDIDATE SCREENING

Efficient screening methods help ensure that only the most suitable candidates move forward in the recruitment process:

- **RESUME SCREENING**
  - Utilize software tools to scan resumes for keywords related to the skills, experience, and qualifications listed in the job description.

- **PHONE SCREENING**
  - Conduct brief phone or video interviews to assess candidates' communication skills, motivation, and salary expectations.

- **ASSESSMENT TOOLS**
  - Implement skills tests, personality assessments, or job simulations as appropriate to further verify candidate qualifications.

CHALLENGES AND COMMON MISTAKES IN SOURCING AND SCREENING INCLUDE:

- **BIAS IN SCREENING**
  - o Unconscious bias can lead to overlooking qualified candidates. Implement structured interview processes and diverse hiring panels to mitigate this risk.

- **INEFFICIENT SOURCING**
  - o Spreading efforts too thinly across too many platforms without a targeted strategy can waste resources and yield poor results.

To overcome these challenges, regularly review and adjust your sourcing and screening techniques based on performance metrics and feedback from hiring managers.

INNOVATIVE ASSESSMENT TECHNIQUES

Once you have gathered a pool of candidates that appear to fit the initial brief, it is time to drill down and see if they truly are the right fit.

- **SKILLS TESTING**
  - o Skills tests tailored to specific roles objectively measure candidate abilities. Automated analysis tools can provide detailed insights, reducing hiring bias and ensuring a fair assessment process.

- **GAMIFICATION**
  - o Incorporating game-based assessments can make the eval-

uation process more engaging. These tools can reveal candidates' problem-solving and communication skills in a playful, less stressful environment.

- **ASYNCHRONOUS INTERVIEWS**
  - Asynchronous interviews allow candidates to record responses to pre-set questions at their convenience. This method offers flexibility, reduces scheduling conflicts, and provides a consistent experience for all candidates.

- **PAID TAKE-HOME ASSIGNMENTS**
  - Assignments related to real work tasks can showcase candidates' abilities and work ethic. Paying candidates for their time demonstrates respect for their effort and can enhance their interest in the role.

- **AI-POWERED ASSESSMENTS**
  - AI tools can grade candidate responses to open-ended questions, analyze speech, and extract insights about personalities and skills. This technology saves time and reduces bias, ensuring a fairer hiring process.

[
"In today's rapidly evolving job market, companies that embrace innovative recruitment strategies stand out from the competition."
]

ACTION STEPS

HOW TO APPLY THE INSIGHTS FROM THIS CHAPTER

- Integrate AI-powered chatbots on your career page to answer candidate questions, provide additional information, and guide applicants through the process. Ensure to maintain human touchpoints for a personalized experience.

- Develop and implement skills tests tailored to specific roles to objectively measure candidate abilities. Use automated analysis tools to reduce hiring bias and ensure fair assessments.

- Organize in-person or hybrid recruitment events to directly connect with candidates, showcase your company culture, and enhance your employer branding.

KEY TAKEAWAY

Effective candidate sourcing and screening are pivotal in finding the right talent. By employing diverse sourcing strategies and thorough screening processes, new talent leaders can significantly enhance their recruitment efficacy. Remember, the goal is not just to fill positions but to find candidates who will thrive and contribute to the organization's long-term success.

Adopting innovative recruitment strategies is no longer optional in today's competitive job market. By embracing creativity and technology, companies can enhance the candidate experience, attract and assess top talent, and build a stronger employer brand. As a talent leader, your role is to spearhead these changes, ensuring your organization remains at the forefront of the recruitment landscape. Embrace innovation, and watch your hiring process transform, bringing in the best talent to drive your company's success.

gocorneroffice.com

CHAPTER 5

MASTERING THE INTERVIEW: INNOVATIVE TECHNIQUES FOR UNCOVERING TOP TALENT

INTERVIEWING TECHNIQUES

Interviewing is like an art and a science blended together, needing a mix of people skills and structured methods to truly gauge if a candidate is the right fit. For talent leaders, nailing down great interview techniques is key to choosing the perfect candidate who not only meets the job needs but also vibes with the company's culture and values.

THE ART AND SCIENCE OF EFFECTIVE INTERVIEWING

Interviewing effectively involves understanding human behavior, psychology, and applying structured methodologies to gather consistent and relevant information about candidates.

- **BUILDING RAPPORT**
  - The art of interviewing begins with creating a comfortable environment for candidates to openly discuss their experiences and skills.

- **BEHAVIORAL QUESTIONS**
  - ○ Asking candidates to describe past professional situations helps interviewers predict future behavior and performance.

REVAMPING YOUR INTERVIEW PROCESS

The conventional question-and-answer interview format is quickly becoming outdated as companies strive for more effective ways to evaluate candidates. Traditional interviews often fail to reveal a candidate's true capabilities and compatibility with the organization. To address this, forward-thinking companies are adopting innovative interview techniques that offer a comprehensive view of candidates' skills, personalities, and cultural fit. This chapter explores these cutting-edge methods and provides actionable strategies for updating your company's interview process.

INNOVATIVE INTERVIEW TECHNIQUES

BEHAVIORAL EVENT INTERVIEWING (BEI)

Behavioral Event Interviewing (BEI) focuses on evaluating a candidate's past actions in specific situations rather than hypothetical ones. This approach gives insight into how candidates have handled real-life challenges and demonstrates their problem-solving abilities.

EXAMPLE BEI QUESTIONS

Think about a time when you identified a process or system inefficiency at work. What actions did you take to address it, and what were the results?

- This question assesses the candidate's problem-solving skills, initiative, and ability to improve processes.

  Describe an instance when you had to deliver difficult feedback to a colleague or subordinate. How did you approach the conversation, and what was the outcome?

- This question assesses the candidate's ability to communicate effectively, demonstrate empathy, and manage delicate situations.

  Recall a situation where you set a challenging goal for yourself or your team. What steps did you take to achieve it, and what were the results?

- This question focuses on the candidate's goal-setting abilities, determination, and success in achieving objectives.

CASE-BASED INTERVIEWS

Case-based interviews, commonly used in fields like consulting and finance, present candidates with real or hypothetical business scenarios. Candidates analyze the situation, identify key issues, and propose solutions, demonstrating their analytical and critical thinking skills.

EXAMPLE CASE-BASED INTERVIEW QUESTIONS

Your company is facing declining sales in a key product line. You have been tasked with identifying the root cause and developing a strategy to reverse the trend. How would you approach this problem, and what steps would you take to implement your solution?

- This question evaluates the candidate's analytical thinking, strategic planning, and problem-solving skills.

   Imagine you are leading a team on a project with a strict deadline, and one of your key team members suddenly becomes unavailable due to an emergency. How would you handle this situation to ensure the project stays on track?

- This question assesses the candidate's leadership, adaptability, and crisis management abilities.

   Your organization is planning to enter a new market, but there is significant competition and regulatory challenges. How would you conduct a market analysis, and what key factors would you consider to make a recommendation on whether to proceed or not?

- This question focuses on the candidate's market research skills, strategic decision-making, and ability to navigate complex business environments.

ROLE-PLAYING EXERCISES

Role-playing exercises immerse candidates in simulated scenarios relevant to the role they are applying for. This technique evaluates practical skills, interpersonal dynamics, and how candidates handle real-time challenges.

> "Interviewing is like an art and a science blended together."

EXAMPLE ROLE-PLAYING EXERCISES

- **CUSTOMER COMPLAINT RESOLUTION**
  - ○ **SCENARIO:** You are a customer service representative at a tech company. A customer calls in, frustrated because their recently purchased device is malfunctioning. They are demanding a refund but are also open to a replacement if handled correctly.

  - ○ **ROLE-PLAYING TASK:** As the candidate, handle the call with the interviewer acting as the upset customer. Focus on understanding the customer's issue, calming their frustration, and providing a satisfactory resolution, whether it's troubleshooting the device, offering a replacement, or processing a refund.

- **TEAM CONFLICT MEDIATION**
  - ○ **SCENARIO:** You are a team leader, and two of your team members are in conflict over the direction of a project. Their disagreement is causing delays and tension within the team.

  - ○ **ROLE-PLAYING TASK:** Mediate a meeting between the two team members, with the interviewer playing the roles of both employees. Demonstrate your conflict resolution skills by facilitating a productive conversation, identifying the root cause of the disagreement, and helping the team members find a mutually agreeable solution.

- **SALES PITCH TO A POTENTIAL CLIENT**
  - ○ **SCENARIO:** You are a sales executive at a marketing firm. You have a meeting with a potential client who is considering your firm for their next major advertising campaign. The client is interested but has concerns about the budget and ROI.

○ **ROLE-PLAYING TASK:** Conduct a sales pitch to the interviewer acting as the potential client. Highlight the strengths of your firm, address the client's concerns about budget and ROI, and try to persuade them to choose your firm for their campaign. Demonstrate your sales techniques, knowledge of the industry, and ability to handle objections.

PORTFOLIO REVIEWS

For roles that require specific tangible skills, such as graphic design or writing, portfolio reviews allow candidates to showcase their work. This approach provides evidence of their abilities and facilitates discussions about their creative processes and problem-solving skills.

EXAMPLE PORTFOLIO REVIEW QUESTIONS

Can you walk us through one of your most challenging projects in your portfolio? What was the project about, what obstacles did you face, and how did you overcome them?

- This question evaluates the candidate's problem-solving abilities, creativity, and resilience in handling difficult projects.

Which project in your portfolio are you most proud of and why? What were your key contributions, and what impact did the project have?

- This question assesses the candidate's sense of achievement, specific skills, and the value they bring to their work.

Choose a project from your portfolio that required significant collaboration with others. How did you manage the teamwork aspect, and what strategies did you use to ensure successful collaboration?

- This question focuses on the candidate's teamwork and communication skills, as well as their ability to work effectively in a collaborative environment.

GROUP INTERVIEWS AND COLLABORATIVE TASKS

Group interviews and collaborative tasks assess candidates' teamwork, communication, and leadership skills. Observing candidates in group settings provides insights into their ability to interact with others and contribute to collective goals.

EXAMPLE GROUP INTERVIEW EXERCISES

- **GROUP PROBLEM-SOLVING TASK**
  - **SCENARIO:** The group is given a business problem to solve, such as developing a strategy to increase market share for a declining product line.

  - **EXERCISE:** Each candidate will discuss their ideas and work together to come up with a comprehensive plan. The focus will be on how candidates communicate, collaborate, and contribute to finding a solution. They should demonstrate their ability to listen, negotiate, and build on each other's ideas.

- **ROLE PLAY WITH MULTIPLE ROLES**
  - **SCENARIO:** The group is tasked with planning a major event

for the company, such as a product launch. Each candidate is assigned a specific role (e.g., event coordinator, marketing manager, logistics manager, finance manager).

○ **EXERCISE:** Candidates must work together to outline the key steps for the event, allocate responsibilities, and address potential challenges. The focus will be on leadership, organization, role-specific knowledge, and the ability to collaborate effectively under time constraints.

● **CASE STUDY ANALYSIS**
   ○ **SCENARIO:** The group is provided with a detailed case study about a company facing a significant issue, such as a public relations crisis or a sudden drop in sales.

   ○ **EXERCISE:** Candidates must analyze the case study together, identify the main issues, and propose a strategic plan to address them. They will then present their findings and recommendations as a group. This exercise evaluates analytical thinking, teamwork, presentation skills, and the ability to think critically under pressure.

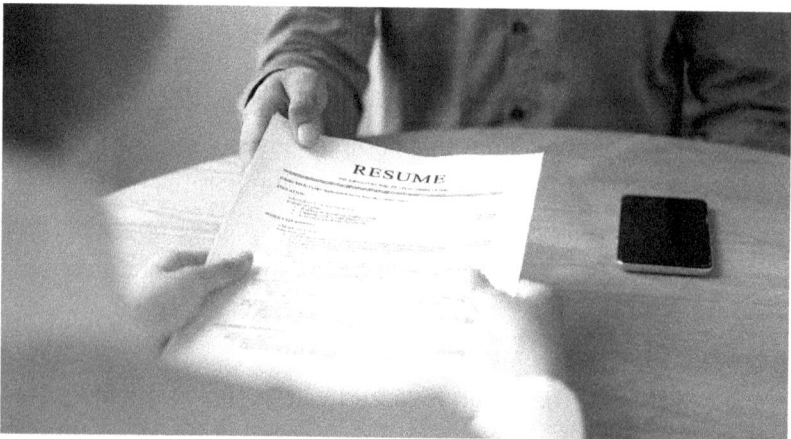

STRESS INTERVIEWS

Stress interviews are designed to evaluate how candidates handle pressure and uncertainty. While not suitable for every role, this technique can reveal important aspects of a candidate's personality and resilience.

EXAMPLE STRESS INTERVIEW QUESTIONS

Why do you think you are better than the other candidates we are interviewing?

- This question puts the candidate on the spot to justify their unique qualifications and strengths under pressure.

Can you describe a time when you failed at something significant? How did you handle it, and what did you learn from the experience?

- This question requires the candidate to reflect on a past failure and discuss it openly, testing their ability to stay composed and introspective.

If we were to ask your previous employer about your biggest weakness, what would they say?

- This question pushes the candidate to confront and articulate their perceived weaknesses while maintaining confidence and self-awareness.

[*"...nailing down great interview techniques is key to choosing the perfect candidate."*]

IMPLEMENTING INNOVATIVE TECHNIQUES

- **TRAINING INTERVIEWERS**
  - Ensure that interviewers are well-versed in the chosen techniques and understand how to evaluate responses effectively. Training equips interviewers with the skills to ask insightful follow-up questions and interpret candidate responses with nuance.

- **CONSISTENCY ACROSS CANDIDATES**
  - Maintain consistency in applying techniques across all candidates to ensure a fair and unbiased evaluation. This enhances the reliability of the assessment process.

- **ALIGNING WITH ORGANIZATIONAL VALUES**
  - Tailor the chosen techniques to align with your organization's values and the specific requirements of the role. This ensures that the evaluation process reflects the attributes crucial for success within your company.

- **ENHANCING CANDIDATE EXPERIENCE**
  - Create a positive candidate experience, even when using unconventional techniques. Clear communication about the interview format and opportunities for candidates to showcase their strengths contribute to a positive impression of your organization.

"Stress interviews are designed to evaluate how candidates handle pressure and uncertainty."

LEVERAGING TECHNOLOGY IN TALENT ACQUISITION

- **GENERATIVE AI**
  - Generative AI can assist in writing job descriptions, crafting interview questions, and communicating with candidates. This technology personalizes candidate outreach and streamlines the recruitment process.

- **REAL-TIME FEEDBACK TOOLS**
  - AI tools can collect and analyze real-time candidate feedback, helping to refine the interview process and improve the candidate experience.

- **BLOCKCHAIN FOR BACKGROUND CHECKS**
  - Blockchain technology can securely streamline background screening and credential verification, reducing administrative burdens and enhancing trust in the hiring process.

- **TALENT INTELLIGENCE**
  - Talent intelligence assesses skills adjacency, enabling the identification of candidates who may not have direct experience but possess the core skills required for the role. This approach broadens the talent pool and mitigates bias.

- **INTERVIEW REPORTING USING AI**
  - Using an AI tool to record and analyze an interview can be a useful way of reassessing a candidate's answers and to see their interactions and participation after the fact. It is also an invaluable tool for anyone in the recruitment team who was unable to attend to assess the candidate without the need for additional appointments.

INTERVIEW FEEDBACK FLOWCHART

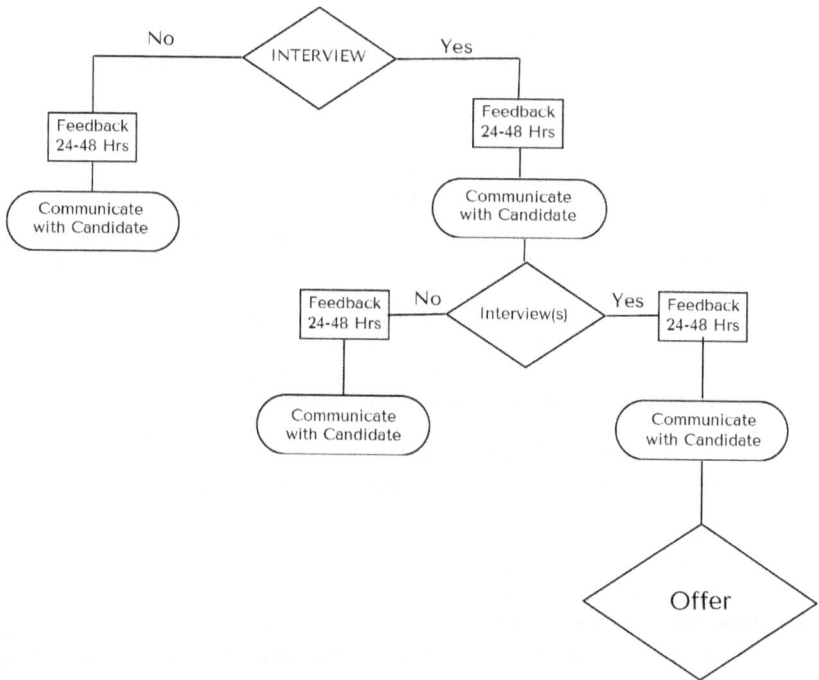

In addition to Interview Feedback Flowchart, a weekly cadence call should occur providing updates, insights, submittals and recommendations.

KEY TAKEAWAY

Effective interviewing is crucial for hiring success. By implementing structured interview techniques, alongside innovative interview techniques, talent leaders can make more informed decisions, reduce biases, and ensure a fair evaluation process.

Updating your company's interview questions and processes with innovative techniques can significantly improve your ability to assess candidates' true potential. By adopting methods like BEI, case-based interviews, role-playing exercises, portfolio reviews, group interviews, and stress interviews, you can gain a comprehensive understanding of candidates' skills and suitability. Leveraging technology further enhances the efficiency and effectiveness of your talent acquisition efforts. Embrace these innovations to build a dynamic and successful workforce this year and beyond.

gocorneroffice.com

CHAPTER 6

TALENT TRAILBLAZERS: PROACTIVE STRATEGIES FOR RECRUITMENT MASTERY

Navigating the labyrinth of talent acquisition requires more than just knowledge—it demands a proactive stance and a mastery of strategic maneuvers. This chapter outlines a straightforward yet comprehensive path to success in hiring, emphasizing the importance of owning the process and adopting a proactive approach.

OWNING THE RECRUITMENT PROCESS

- **EMPOWERMENT THROUGH OWNERSHIP**
  - Start by fostering a sense of ownership among talent acquisition professionals. Encourage them to view themselves as strategic partners in the business rather than just facilitators.

- **EXPERTISE PROMOTION**
  - Highlighting the significance of elevating internal expertise to hiring managers involves more than just presenting skills and achievements. It also entails educating hiring teams on the strategic value of talent acquisition. A crucial aspect is demonstrating that talent acquisition success should not be

gauged by cost savings per hire, but by the ability to provide a feasible plan to mitigate the upheaval when a leader exits without a proper succession strategy in place. Display this comprehension by actively engaging in the market to cultivate a potential pipeline of leaders and other pivotal roles.

- **YOUR SEAT AT THE TABLE**
  - The seat should not be a silent one; instead, it should offer a chance to champion a forward-thinking strategy for succession and talent management. Encourage leaders to outline their exit strategy: will their successor be an internal promotion, or is there a need to cultivate a pipeline for the future? Inquire about actions taken to support this strategy over the past year.

STRATEGIC ALIGNMENT WITH BUSINESS GOALS

- **LINKING TALENT TO OBJECTIVES**
  - Discussing the alignment of recruitment strategies with broader business objectives is crucial. This alignment guarantees that each hiring decision contributes to the company's long-term goals.

- **CONSULTATIVE ROLE OF RECRUITERS**
  - Explore the role of recruiters as business consultants, providing valuable insights into market dynamics, the talent pool, and competitive salary structures to drive organizational success.

["Navigating the labyrinth of talent acquisition requires more than just knowledge."]

PROACTIVE RECRUITMENT TACTICS

- **PREDICTIVE HIRING**
  - By utilizing data and analytics, companies can forecast their hiring requirements proactively, preventing them from becoming urgent. This forward-thinking strategy enables companies to operate strategically rather than reactively.

- **TALENT POOLING**
  - Developing a method to create and sustain a talent pool involves nurturing relationships with potential candidates even before a specific need arises. It's about fostering connections and building a network of skilled individuals for future opportunities.

BEST PRACTICES FOR IMPLEMENTATION

- **STRUCTURED ONBOARDING**
  - A comprehensive onboarding process that starts prior to the new employee's first day and extends throughout their initial year to promote integration and retention efforts is crucial for organizational success.

- **CONTINUOUS LEARNING AND DEVELOPMENT**
  - Implement programs that foster continuous learning and skill development, ensuring that the workforce remains adaptable and responsive to evolving industry trends and demands.

["Start by fostering a sense of ownership among talent acquisition professionals."]

CHALLENGES AND SOLUTIONS

- **SCALABILITY ISSUES**
  - ○ Address the common scalability challenges in talent acquisition by providing effective solutions tailored to meet the needs of expanding businesses.

- **MAINTAINING QUALITY DURING RAPID GROWTH**
  - ○ Provide effective strategies for upholding hiring standards and preserving organizational culture amidst phases of rapid growth.

ACTION STEPS

HOW TO APPLY THE INSIGHTS FROM THIS CHAPTER

- Create a checklist for aligning recruitment practices with business objectives.

- Develop a plan for promoting talent acquisition's strategic value within your organization.

- Initiate a pilot project for a predictive hiring model based on historical data and projected growth.

KEY TAKEAWAY

The journey to achieving successful hiring is multifaceted and demands a proactive, strategic approach. By assuming responsibility for the recruitment process and closely aligning with business objectives, talent acquisition professionals can markedly boost their effectiveness and make valuable contributions to the organization's overall success.

gocorneroffice.com

CHAPTER 7

COMMUNICATION UNLEASHED: MASTERING THE ART OF TALENT ACQUISITION DIALOGUE

Effective communication is not just about sharing information—it's about creating an environment where information flows seamlessly between all parties involved in the hiring process. This chapter explores how to establish and control a robust communication framework that facilitates successful talent acquisition.

ESTABLISHING CLEAR COMMUNICATION PROTOCOLS

- **SETTING EXPECTATIONS EARLY**
  - Begin the recruitment process by clearly defining roles, responsibilities, and expectations for both recruiters and hiring managers. This prevents misunderstandings and sets the stage for a smooth collaboration.

- **COMMUNICATION CADENCE**
  - Develop a regular communication schedule that keeps all stakeholders informed and engaged throughout the hiring process. This includes regular updates, feedback sessions, and strategic planning meetings.

EFFECTIVE TOOLS FOR COMMUNICATION

- **DIGITAL PLATFORMS**
  - Leverage technology to streamline communication. Tools like applicant tracking systems (ATS) and human resource information systems (HRIS) can facilitate the efficient flow of information.

- **FEEDBACK MECHANISMS**
  - Implement structured feedback mechanisms that allow for continuous improvement. This includes both internal feedback from the recruitment team and external feedback from candidates.

OPTIMIZING COMMUNICATION WITH CANDIDATES

- **TRANSPARENCY WITH APPLICANTS**
  - Maintain a transparent communication line with candidates about the status of their applications, what they can expect next, and feedback from interviews.

- **BUILDING RELATIONSHIPS**
  - Utilize effective communication to cultivate relationships with candidates, prioritizing their sense of value and respect throughout the entire process, irrespective of the final outcome.

TRAINING AND DEVELOPMENT FOR EFFECTIVE COMMUNICATION

- **SKILL DEVELOPMENT WORKSHOPS**
  - ○ Organize regular training sessions for the HR and recruitment team focusing on honing effective communication skills. This includes instruction on negotiation, persuasive communication, and fostering emotional intelligence.

- **BEST PRACTICES SHARING**
  - ○ Establish interactive forums where team members can collaboratively share successful communication strategies, fostering a culture of knowledge exchange and learning from each other's experiences.

ADDRESSING COMMUNICATION CHALLENGES

- **CROSS-CULTURAL COMMUNICATION**
  - ○ Offer advice on effectively handling cross-cultural communication, particularly within a global recruitment setting.

- **HANDLING DIFFICULT CONVERSATIONS**
  - ○ Provide tactics for managing difficult conversations, like negotiating offers, conveying rejections, or addressing delicate subjects.

"Begin the recruitment process by clearly defining roles, responsibilities, and expectations for both recruiters and hiring managers."

ACTION STEPS

HOW TO APPLY THE INSIGHTS FROM THIS CHAPTER

- Audit your existing communication tools and strategies to pinpoint areas that can be enhanced.

- Implement one new communication tool or strategy aimed at enhancing transparency with candidates.

- Organize a workshop on effective communication skills tailored for your recruitment team.

KEY TAKEAWAY

Controlling the communication framework within talent acquisition is absolutely vital for boosting efficiency and achieving success. Through the establishment of clear protocols, the use of effective tools, and the ongoing development of communication skills, organizations have a great opportunity to enhance their recruitment results and elevate the experiences of candidates.

gocorneroffice.com

CHAPTER 8

TIME IS TALENT: MASTERING SPEED AND TRANSPARENCY IN RECRUITMENT

In the highly competitive realm of talent acquisition, time plays a pivotal role. This chapter delves into the vital realm of timeline management and transparent communication with candidates, underscoring the importance of swift action and fostering open dialogue. By acting promptly and upholding clear channels of communication, we ensure top candidates remain engaged and dedicated.

UNDERSTANDING CANDIDATE BEHAVIOR

- **MARKET AWARENESS**
  - Acknowledge that top talent frequently has numerous choices. Comprehend the intricacies of candidate behavior in competitive markets, where candidates are prone to interact with various prospective employers.

- **IMPORTANCE OF SPEED**
  - Emphasize the significance of swift, responsive communication to present a compelling offer ahead of competitors.

STREAMLINING THE RECRUITMENT PROCESS

- **EFFICIENCY IN PROCESSES**
  - Identify bottlenecks in the recruitment process that slow down decision-making and candidate progression. Implement strategies to enhance process efficiency, such as reducing unnecessary steps and improving coordination between departments.

- **USE OF TECHNOLOGY**
  - Discuss the integration of recruitment technologies that enable faster screening, assessment, and communication with candidates.

- **TIMELINES**
  - Can serve as a crucial asset in maintaining the momentum of the recruitment process, underscoring the value of everyone's time.

To maintain the momentum and efficiency of your operations, it's crucial to distinguish between speed and timeliness. A concise and well-timed process hinges on seamless schedule coordination and purpose-driven interviews. Conversely, a more extended process can be equally effective if the expectations and objectives align with the hiring criteria.

Take Chick-fil-A, for example. They view their hiring process as akin to a courtship before the proposal stage, which typically involves 6–8 interviews over several months. While this may seem exhaustive and overly drawn out, delving into candidates' personalities, knowledge, and breadth of experience ensures a comprehensive understanding.

EFFECTIVE COMMUNICATION WITH CANDIDATES

- **IMMEDIATE ACKNOWLEDGMENT**
  - ○ Ensure that every candidate receives an immediate acknowledgment of their application, setting a positive tone for future interactions.

- **REGULAR UPDATES**
  - ○ Establish a protocol for providing candidates with regular updates throughout the recruitment process, even when there is no new information, to keep them engaged and informed. Keep in mind, beyond just fulfilling the role, it's important that every candidate has a positive experience to enhance your employment brand and future opportunities.

BUILDING A CANDIDATE-CENTRIC APPROACH

- **RESPECT FOR CANDIDATE TIME**
  - ○ Highlighting the significance of valuing candidates' time involves scheduling interviews and other communications at mutually convenient times and ensuring punctuality.

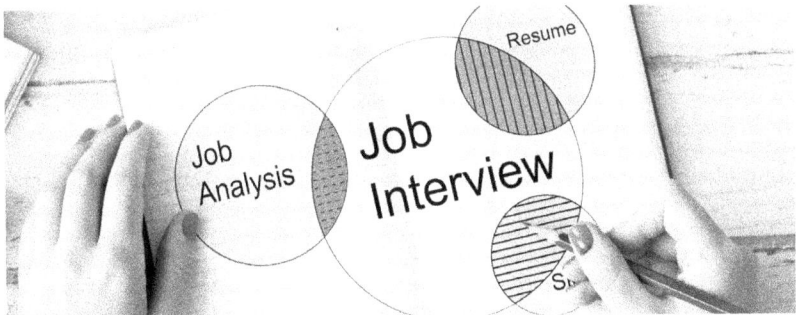

- **FEEDBACK AND ENGAGEMENT**
  - Offer valuable, constructive, and timely feedback post-interviews. Engage candidates by sharing insights on company culture, the role's significance, and growth prospects within the organization.

HANDLING MULTIPLE OFFERS AND NEGOTIATIONS

- **TRANSPARENCY IN NEGOTIATIONS**
  - Encourage an open and transparent discussion throughout the recruitment process, which may involve the possibility of receiving multiple offers from various organizations. Ask and check in with candidates continuously throughout the interview process to find out if they have any other offers, whether your company is their top choice, and their compensation expectations, as well as how these align with the hiring team's expectations for an offer.

- **COUNTEROFFER STRATEGIES**
  - Prepare for and strategically handle counteroffers and last-minute negotiations to secure top talent. Be sure to address the conversation of counter offers with each candidate and remind them of their "why" for interviewing.

As a company, we ensure to address compensation with candidates right from the initial conversation. It is our philosophy to engage in open and transparent dialogues. This approach nurtures the opportunity to pose questions, assess the responses, and ensure that it is a suitable match for the candidate.

When faced with resistance during discussions on compensation, it is not about undervaluing individuals but rather about ensuring alignment. While conversations about compensation can be difficult, addressing them proactively leads to the best possible results.

["In the highly competitive realm of talent acquisition, time plays a pivotal role."]

ACTION STEPS

HOW TO APPLY THE INSIGHTS FROM THIS CHAPTER

- Review and refine your communication protocols with candidates to ensure they are streamlined and candidate-friendly.

- Train your recruitment team on the importance of timeline management and effective negotiation techniques.

- Implement at least one technological solution that reduces time-to-hire by automating parts of the recruitment process.

KEY TAKEAWAY

Timeliness and transparency play a crucial role in attracting the best talent in a competitive job market. By refining communication and negotiation tactics, as well as valuing the candidate's journey during the recruitment process, companies can boost their attractiveness to top-tier candidates and elevate their overall recruitment achievements.

gocorneroffice.com

CHAPTER 9

CANDIDATE FIRST: CRAFTING UNFORGETTABLE RECRUITMENT EXPERIENCES

The candidate experience plays a crucial role in the recruitment process, profoundly impacting an organization's reputation (employment branding) and its capacity to draw in top talent. This chapter thoroughly explores strategies aimed at crafting a positive and lasting candidate experience, guaranteeing that candidates feel genuinely valued and respected throughout their journey, irrespective of the hiring result.

FOUNDATIONS OF A POSITIVE CANDIDATE EXPERIENCE

- **CLEAR COMMUNICATION**
  - Stress the importance of clear, timely, and respectful communication from the initial contact through to the final decision.

- **TRANSPARENCY**
  - Maintain transparency about the recruitment process, expectations, and timelines to build trust and respect with candidates.

ENHANCING THE INTERVIEW PROCESS

- **PREPARATION AND RESPECT**
  - Ensure that all interviewers are well-prepared, respectful, and punctual. The professionalism displayed during interviews reflects the organization's overall culture.

- **CONSISTENCY AND FAIRNESS**
  - Implement standardized interview procedures to guarantee fairness and consistency in how candidates are evaluated.

- **TIMELINE**
  - Share the expected timeline with all parties from hiring managers to candidates. Everybody stays positive when they know the expectations and that the expectations are met.

EXAMPLE: The candidate has a great interview with the hiring manager. However, the next scheduled round's interviewer gets called away for something urgent, causing a delay, this is not shared with the candidate in an open way . Effective communication is key to keeping the candidate engaged. Without updates, the candidate's enthusiasm wanes, leading to doubts and eventually, losing interest in the company. This results in a missed opportunity and damages the company's employment branding reputation. Clear communication could have easily prevented this costly outcome.

FEEDBACK AND FOLLOW-UP

- **CONSTRUCTIVE FEEDBACK**
  - Provide constructive feedback to candidates post-interview, offering insights that can aid their professional growth, regardless of the hiring decision.

> "Be kind, not nice. Nice is when you care more about how they will feel about you. Kind is when you care more about them."

By not providing constructive feedback you hinder the candidate's opportunities of moving forward with your process or any future process. A good way to start the conversation is "Candidate, I really enjoy working with you and from the onset I shared that I will provide feedback as I believe you are professional and will be able to build on all aspects good and bad. Here is what has been shared..."

- **ONGOING ENGAGEMENT**
  - For applicants who are not chosen, explore ways to sustain their interest. This could involve adding them to a talent pool for upcoming roles or offering networking guidance.

RESPECT FOR THE CANDIDATE'S JOURNEY

- **UNDERSTANDING PERSONAL INVESTMENT**
  - Acknowledge the effort and time candidates invest in applying and interviewing, and respect this commitment by making the process as smooth and stress-free as possible.

- **CLOSURE AND APPRECIATION**
  - It is important to ensure that every candidate is provided with a clear and respectful conclusion to their application process. Express gratitude for their interest and efforts, showing appreciation for the time they invested in the opportunity.

INCORPORATING CANDIDATE FEEDBACK

- **FEEDBACK SURVEYS**
  - It is important to consistently seek feedback from candidates regarding their experience, leveraging this valuable information to iteratively enhance the recruitment process.

- **ADAPTIVE STRATEGIES**
  - Adjust the recruitment strategies by incorporating candidate feedback to effectively align with the expectations and requirements of potential applicants. Growth stems from experiences and can add strength to your approach and employer brand.

> "The candidate experience plays a crucial role in the recruitment process, profoundly impacting an organization's reputation (employment branding) and its capacity to draw in top talent."

ACTION STEPS

HOW TO APPLY THE INSIGHTS FROM THIS CHAPTER

- Implement a standardized feedback mechanism that provides valuable insights to all interviewed candidates.

- Conduct quarterly reviews of the interview process and candidate feedback to identify areas for improvement.

- Try out new procedures and gather feedback from the candidates.

KEY TAKEAWAY

A positive candidate experience is vital not just for attracting the best talent, but also for crafting a robust employer brand that connects with professionals in your field. By dedicating resources to respectful and engaging recruitment processes, companies can guarantee that each candidate transforms into a potential brand ambassador, grateful for the experience they had irrespective of the hiring decision.

gocorneroffice.com

CHAPTER 10

CLOSING THE DEAL: ENSURING SMOOTH OFFERS AND STELLAR ONBOARDING

Securing a candidate's acceptance marks a pivotal moment in the recruitment process. This chapter delves into the crucial final steps of securing a new hire, underlining the significance of a smooth offer process and outlining the essential strategies needed to guarantee a successful onboarding experience for the candidate.

FINALIZING THE OFFER

- **CLEAR AND ATTRACTIVE OFFER**
  - Make sure that the offer clearly delineates the role, compensation, benefits, and any other relevant specifics. Strive to enhance its appeal while adhering to organizational policies and market standards.

- **TIMELINESS**
  - Provide the offer promptly post decision-making. Delays may result in losing the candidate to other opportunities.

Our approach is to begin with a verbal offer and to discuss it with the candidate. Since we previously discussed compensation and expectations, negotiations are simple: Offer, Volley, End of Match.

EFFECTIVE NEGOTIATION TECHNIQUES

- **OPEN AND TRANSPARENT**
  - Establishing an open and transparent relationship is crucial. The insights you've acquired pave the way for smoother conversations and negotiations, as much of the compensation would have been addressed beforehand.

- **LOCK THEM IN**
  - Ensure their commitment to the opportunity and the flexible terms of a potential offer before reaching the offer stage.

- **UNDERSTANDING CANDIDATE PRIORITIES**
  - Tailor the negotiation process by understanding what is most important to the candidate—whether it's salary, benefits, flexibility, or professional growth opportunities.

- **HANDLING COUNTEROFFERS**
  - Be prepared to address counteroffers swiftly and effectively. Understand the candidate's concerns and reiterate the benefits of the new role and the career growth opportunities it presents.

- **THERE ARE A FEW THINGS TO KEEP IN MIND WHEN DISCUSSING WITH A CANDIDATE THAT IS CONSIDERING ACCEPTING A COUNTEROFFER**

  - 89% leave on their own within six months or are asked to leave within a year.

○ If the candidate accepts a counteroffer and decides to stay, they should expect there to be a loss of trust in their loyalty and dedication. The original company knows they were interviewed, knows they were interested in leaving, and knows they are only still with them because of money.

● **AN ADDITIONAL QUESTION TO ASK THE CANDIDATE**
○ Why did it take an offer from another company to increase their stake?

ONBOARDING FOR SUCCESS

● **STRUCTURED ONBOARDING PROGRAM**
○ Develop a comprehensive onboarding program that starts from the moment the offer is accepted. This should include a written offer, pre-onboarding communications, a detailed first day and first week agenda, and a clear outline of initial projects and expectations.

● **INTEGRATION WITH THE TEAM**
○ Facilitate early introductions to team members and key stakeholders. Arrange mentorship or buddy systems to help the new hire integrate smoothly into the company culture.

MAINTAINING ENGAGEMENT POST-OFFER

● **COMMUNICATION PRIOR TO START DATE**
○ Keep in touch with the candidate between the acceptance of the offer and the start date. Regular check-ins can help alleviate any concerns and build excitement about the new role.

#5: DON'T FORGET ABOUT ME

An offer is made to a great candidate after months of searching. The hiring team gets background completed and sets a start date for one month later but NEVER contacts the soon-to-be employee again. Big mistake. The candidate reaches out a few times with questions but does not hear back in a timely manner. After three weeks of neglect and no answers before the anticipated start date, the candidate pulls out of the process due to fear that if this is the way they treat employees and the company operates before joining, they don't want any part of that culture.

ACTION STEPS

HOW TO APPLY THE INSIGHTS FROM THIS CHAPTER

- Review and streamline your offer process to ensure it is as efficient and clear as possible.

- Develop an onboarding checklist that covers all aspects from pre-onboarding to the end of the first year.

- Train hiring managers on best practices for handling counteroffers and maintaining engagement with new hires before their start date.

KEY TAKEAWAY

When reaching the end of the recruitment process, it's not just about extending an offer; it's about securing the hire with a considerate strategy and laying the groundwork for sustained success. A meticulously executed final phase not only boosts the new hire's initial experience but also influences their long term engagement and retention within the organization.

gocorneroffice.com

CHAPTER 11

CRISIS CONTROL: TURNING RECRUITMENT SETBACKS INTO SUCCESS

Even the most meticulously planned recruitment strategies may face unforeseen challenges. This chapter dives into adeptly managing setbacks in the recruitment process, ranging from abrupt candidate withdrawals to internal miscommunications, and transforming these hurdles into chances for enhancement.

The Best Practices Checklist which is included in the appendix will alleviate many of the most common recruitment challenges.

IDENTIFYING COMMON RECRUITMENT CHALLENGES

- **UNEXPECTED CANDIDATE WITHDRAWALS**
  - Discover effective approaches for handling scenarios when a leading candidate withdraws unexpectedly towards the end of the selection process.

- **INTERNAL MISCOMMUNICATIONS**
  - Discuss strategies for realigning hiring managers and the recruitment team in case of a disconnect.

- **BUDGET CUTS AND RESTRUCTURING**
  - ○ Offer advice on refining recruitment strategies when faced with unexpected budget reductions or organizational restructuring.

PROACTIVE CRISIS MANAGEMENT

- **BUILDING FLEXIBILITY INTO THE PROCESS**
  - ○ Discuss the importance of having flexible strategies that can adapt to changing circumstances without compromising the quality of recruitment. Make certain to communicate any changes with all parties involved in the recruitment process.

- **RISK ASSESSMENT**
  - ○ Implement regular risk assessments for the recruitment process to identify potential issues before they become problematic.

EFFECTIVE COMMUNICATION DURING CRISIS

- **MAINTAINING TRANSPARENCY**
  - ○ Emphasize the significance of upholding transparency with candidates and internal stakeholders amidst a crisis.

- **CLEAR AND CONSISTENT MESSAGING**
  - ○ Maintain clear, consistent communication aligned with the organization's values, even in challenging situations.

["Even the most meticulously planned recruitment strategies may face unforeseen challenges."]

LEARNING FROM SETBACKS

- **FEEDBACK LOOPS**
  - Create robust feedback loops that include input from all stakeholders to understand the lessons and successes.

- **IMPLEMENTING CHANGES**
  - Leverage feedback to enact adjustments, enhancing processes and averting similar issues down the line.

TOOLS AND TECHNOLOGIES TO AID IN CRISIS MANAGEMENT

- **TECHNOLOGY SOLUTIONS**
  - Recommend technology solutions that can help manage recruitment crisis, such as advanced ATS systems that provide real-time data and analytics.

- **TRAINING PROGRAMS**
  - Suggest training programs for recruitment teams that focus on crisis management and adaptive strategies.

ACTION STEPS

HOW TO APPLY THE INSIGHTS FROM THIS CHAPTER

- Develop a contingency plan that addresses common recruitment challenges.

- Conduct a quarterly review of recruitment processes to identify areas for improvement and update the risk assessment.

- Implement a training module for the recruitment team on crisis management and flexibility in processes.

KEY TAKEAWAY

Recruitment is naturally full of surprises, and being ready for the unforeseen is key. This chapter offers a thorough guide on how to gracefully and efficiently handle recruitment crisis, guaranteeing that your organization can swiftly recover and uphold a robust recruitment stance.

Recruitment

Resume

Job
Analysis

Skill

gocorneroffice.com

CHAPTER 12

REINFORCEMENTS READY: LEVERAGING EXTERNAL AGENCIES FOR RECRUITMENT EXCELLENCE

n the constantly changing world of talent acquisition, leaders within companies continually tackle the challenge of finding the best talent to boost organizational success. However, in this quest, external talent acquisition agencies are often underestimated or seen as a threat to the internal talent team. Yet, they are not just a recruitment option; a great external agency can play a vital strategic role that goes beyond traditional hiring approaches and can be a valuable asset and ally to the internal talent team.

- **EXPERTISE AND SPECIALIZATION ARE KEY**
  - External agencies, with deep talent acquisition know-how, bring valuable experience and industry insights to boost recruitment efforts significantly. Their in-depth grasp of market dynamics, along with a drive for innovation, opens doors to a diverse talent pool beyond traditional recruitment avenues.

- **ORGANIZATIONAL OPTIMIZATION**
  - Contrary to conventional wisdom, the decision to engage external agencies is not solely driven by cost considerations but by a broader vision of organizational optimization. While internal

recruitment endeavors often incur hidden costs—from advertising expenses to the drain on internal resources—partnering with external agencies presents a compelling case for cost-effectiveness. Their streamlined processes, coupled with a laser focus on results, translate into tangible savings and accelerated time-to-hire metrics.

- **EXPANSIVE NETWORKS**
  - Yet, perhaps the most compelling rationale for embracing external agencies lies in the access they afford to top-tier talent. Leveraging their expansive networks and longstanding industry relationships, these agencies possess an unparalleled ability to identify and engage with passive candidates—individuals whose talents may elude conventional recruitment efforts. In a landscape where talent is the ultimate differentiator, this access becomes the cornerstone of sustainable organizational growth.

- **ORGANIZATIONAL AGILITY AND FORESIGHT**
  - Essentially, deciding to engage external agencies goes beyond just recruitment; it represents a strategic partnership based on common goals and mutual success. By promoting the utilization of external know-how, internal talent acquisition leaders position themselves as pioneers of organizational agility and foresight. They indicate a shift from the usual way of doing things, embracing innovation as a driver for competitive advantage in a rapidly changing market

["External agencies...bring valuable experience and industry insights to boost recruitment efforts significantly."]

KEY TAKEAWAY

Partnering with external talent acquisition agencies isn't just about convenience; it's a smart move to access expertise and support that bolsters organizational resilience and growth. It showcases the symbiotic bond between internal visionaries and external specialists—a relationship born in the fires of innovation and steered by a mutual dedication to excellence. As organizations navigate the intricacies of talent acquisition in the 21st century, embracing external expertise could turn out to be their most foresighted investment.

gocorneroffice.com

CHAPTER 13

THE FINAL DECISION: EMPOWERING YOUR RECRUITMENT EVOLUTION

As we bring this guide to a close regarding the transformation of recruitment practices, it is crucial to take a moment to contemplate the valuable lessons acquired and the decisions that await your organization. This chapter is designed to empower leaders in talent acquisition, instilling in them a sense of accountability and providing a well-defined direction to elevate their recruitment procedures.

- **SUMMARIZING KEY INSIGHTS**
  - **EFFECTIVE COMMUNICATION:** Reiterate the importance of maintaining clear and consistent communication throughout the recruitment process, which is foundational to successful hiring.
  - **CANDIDATE EXPERIENCE:** Emphasize the role of a positive candidate experience in building your company's reputation and attracting top talent.
  - **STRATEGIC ALIGNMENT:** Highlight the necessity of aligning recruitment strategies with organizational goals to ensure long-term success.
  - **CRISIS MANAGEMENT:** Stress the value of preparedness and flexibility in handling unexpected challenges in the recruitment process.

- **EMPOWERING ACTION**
  - **COMMITMENT TO IMPROVEMENT:** Encourage leaders to commit to continuous improvement in their recruitment practices, advocating for ongoing training, feedback, and adaptation.
  - **LEVERAGING TECHNOLOGY:** Urge the adoption of advanced technology tools that can streamline processes, enhance communication, and provide valuable insights through data analytics.
  - **FOSTERING TEAM COLLABORATION:** Advocate for stronger collaboration and shared goals between recruiters, hiring managers, and organizational leaders to foster a cohesive approach to talent acquisition.

- **CHALLENGES AND OPPORTUNITIES**
  - **NAVIGATING CHANGE:** Discuss the challenges of implementing change within the recruitment function and strategies for overcoming resistance.
  - **FUTURE TRENDS IN RECRUITMENT:** Provide insight into future trends that could impact recruitment, such as the increasing use of AI and machine learning, and how to prepare for these changes.

> "Reiterate the importance of maintaining clear and consistent communication throughout the recruitment process, which is foundational to successful hiring."

ACTION STEPS

HOW TO APPLY THE INSIGHTS FROM THIS CHAPTER

- Conduct a yearly audit of recruitment practices to identify strengths and areas for improvement.

- Organize quarterly training sessions for the recruitment team on new tools and techniques.

- Set up a cross-departmental committee to ensure recruitment strategies are aligned with overall business objectives.

THE LAST WORD

The journey towards improving recruitment practices is continuous and brimming with chances for development and enhancement. By adopting the strategies outlined in this book, leaders can profoundly influence the success of their organizations and establish a recruitment function that is prepared for the future.

This guide has highlighted the path toward transformative recruitment practices, emphasizing the importance of effective communication, a positive candidate experience, strategic alignment, and crisis management. As we've explored, the key to successful hiring lies in building a robust recruitment framework that fosters collaboration, leverages technology, and adapts to change. By prioritizing continuous improvement and embracing the trends of the future, leaders in talent acquisition can secure the right talent and shape a resilient, high-performing workforce that drives organizational success.

The actionable steps and strategies shared throughout this guide aim to empower you to refine your processes, fortify your teams, and navigate the evolving talent landscape with confidence. Now, it's your choice to implement these strategies, processes, systems and insights, fostering a recruitment culture that not only attracts but also retains the best candidates, ensuring a sustainable competitive edge in the years to come.

> "The journey towards improving recruitment practices is continuous and brimming with chances for development and enhancement."

WORK WITH US

CONTINUOUS IMPROVEMENT JOURNEY

At **CornerOffice**, we remain committed to excellence and innovation in talent acquisition. We believe that by sharing our expertise and guiding you through the intricacies of modern recruitment, we can help you build a resilient and effective talent acquisition framework that supports your organization's goals.

The journey to refining your talent acquisition strategy is continuous. It requires a commitment to collaboration, adaptability, and proactive problem-solving. We hope that the insights, tools, and templates provided in the From Misfires to Hires book series have equipped you with the knowledge to elevate your talent acquisition processes.

Thank you for joining us on this journey to supercharge your talent acquisition strategy. We look forward to continuing to support you as you build stronger teams, drive sustainable growth, and achieve recruitment excellence in your organization.

ADDITIONAL SUPPORT

Why stop here? At **CornerOffice**, we understand that implementing these strategies can sometimes require a tailored approach, specific to your organization's unique needs and challenges. That's where **CornerOffice** comes in.

Our team of experienced consultants is ready to partner with you to turn these strategies into action. Here's how we can help:

- **CUSTOMIZED STRATEGY IMPLEMENTATION**
  - We work with your HR and Talent Acquisition teams to tailor and implement the processes, systems, and strategies outlined in this book, ensuring they align perfectly with your organizational goals.

- **PHONE CONSULTATIONS**
  - Need advice or a quick consultation? Our experts are available for one-on-one phone consultations to address specific challenges, provide guidance, and offer solutions tailored to your immediate needs.

- **IN-PERSON CONSULTING**
  - For a more hands-on approach, we offer in-person consulting sessions where our team collaborates with yours on-site to develop and execute a comprehensive talent acquisition strategy.

- **WORKSHOPS AND TRAINING**
  - We provide workshops and training sessions to upskill your team, ensuring they are well-versed in the latest talent acquisition trends, tools, and techniques."

By partnering with **CornerOffice**, you're not just adopting a set of strategies—you're aligning with a team that has a proven track record of achieving a 91%+ retention rate within the first two years of employment for our clients. We're here to ensure that your talent acquisition function is a powerful, strategic driver of success.

Ready to elevate your talent acquisition strategy? Contact us today to schedule a consultation and discover how we can help your organization attract, hire, and retain the right talent. **Visit www.goCorner-Office.com/consulting** or call us at **843.790.6780** to get started. Let's supercharge your team together!

As a special offer for readers of the *From Misfires to Hires* series, we are offering a free 30-minute consultation to discuss how we can help your organization implement the strategies covered in our books. Reach out to us today to claim this offer!

gocorneroffice.com

ABOUT CORNER OFFICE

PIONEERING EXCELLENCE IN TALENT ACQUISITION

At **CornerOffice**, we are more than just an executive search firm—we are your strategic partners in talent acquisition. With decades of combined experience, our mission is to empower CHROs and Talent Acquisition leaders with the tools and expertise to assess, disrupt, and innovate their talent acquisition strategies—resulting in higher retention of top talent. Guided by our core values of Integrity, Loyalty, Generosity, and Excellence, we are committed to forming genuine partnerships and connecting top-tier talent with opportunities that foster mutual growth and success.

EXPERTISE AND COMMITMENT TO EXCELLENCE

CornerOffice's reputation for excellence is built on a foundation of innovative strategies and a personalized approach to talent acquisition. Our proprietary processes and advanced systems have consistently achieved a remarkable 91%+ retention rate within the first two years of employment. This success is a testament to our dedication to understanding the unique cultures, values, and needs of our client partners.

For over a decade, **CornerOffice** has filled thousands of corporate functional positions across various sectors, including Human Resources, Marketing, Sales, E-commerce, Supply Chain, Corporate Strategy, Data Science, Business Development, Finance, Customer Service, and Technology. Our expertise spans industries such as consumer goods, food and beverage, retail, pharmaceuticals, distribution, insurance, property management, manufacturing, and start-ups.

Our team of seasoned talent acquisition experts excels in creating tailored recruitment solutions. We leverage cutting-edge technologies, including advanced AI and machine learning tools, to enhance candidate matching and streamline the hiring process. Our comprehensive assessments ensure that we identify the most suitable candidates for your organization.

IMMERSIVE AND PERSONALIZED APPROACH

What sets **CornerOffice** apart is our commitment to immersion and understanding. We take the time to delve deep into your company's culture, values, and goals. This approach has earned us glowing testimonials from industry leaders. The Regional VP of HR at Sonepar praises our ability to "identify amazing talent and turn it around quickly," while the Talent Acquisition Leader at Chick-fil-A highlights our unique ability to "immerse and understand our company, values, and culture firsthand."

BUILDING LASTING PARTNERSHIPS

At **CornerOffice**, we believe in the power of strong communication and lasting partnerships. Our success is demonstrated by long-term relationships with leading Fortune 500 companies and globally recognized brands across many industries. We are proud to have supported nationally admired organizations in building world-class teams that align with their strategic goals.

Our commitment extends beyond meeting hiring needs—we treat every candidate with respect and ensure a seamless, transparent recruitment process that benefits both candidates and employers. With over a decade of experience and industry-leading retention rates, **CornerOffice** delivers results that drive growth and sustainability for our clients and their businesses.

SHARING KNOWLEDGE FOR SUCCESS

Our latest endeavor, encapsulated in the book *From Misfires to Hires: How You Can Supercharge Your Talent Acquisition Team*, reflects our commitment to sharing our expertise. This comprehensive guide provides CHROs and Talent Acquisition leaders with actionable strategies to enhance their recruitment processes. By emphasizing effective communication, strategic alignment, and innovative techniques, we aim to help our partners build robust talent acquisition functions that support their corporate strategies and attract top right-fit talent. This series underscores our commitment to sharing expertise, emphasizing effective communication, strategic alignment, and innovative techniques to build robust and successful talent acquisition functions that ensure a competitive edge in the marketplace.

FUTURE VISION

Looking ahead, **CornerOffice** remains dedicated to driving innovation in talent acquisition. Our goal is to continue equipping leaders with the insights and tools necessary to navigate the evolving talent landscape. By fostering a culture of continuous improvement and excellence, we strive to be the go-to resource for organizations seeking to elevate their talent acquisition strategies.

To further elevate in supercharging your talent team and strategies, we offer additional resources and individual consulting. Please feel free to contact us: **www.goCornerOffice.com**

In a competitive market, **CornerOffice** stands as a beacon of expertise, reliability, and innovation. Let us help you build a talent acquisition strategy that not only meets but exceeds your organizational goals. Partner with **CornerOffice** and experience the difference that true expertise and commitment can make.

Achieve 91% Retention
Best Practices Checklist

corner office

Communication Protocol

- [ ] Intake/Expectation call with hiring team
- [ ] Weekly update call with Corporate HR/Hiring Manager
- [ ] The Following is **Most EFFECTIVE** for Hiring Manager
  - [ ] Access/Response (24-48 hrs)
  - [ ] Feedback regarding candidates (24-48 hrs)
  - [ ] Timely actions
  - [ ] Potential pivots
- [ ] Offer/Placement

Candidate Experience

- [ ] **Communication** and **Timely** response
- [ ] Defined interview process/schedule
  - [ ] Timeline/dates
- [ ] Honest feedback
- [ ] Offer/Placement

Implementation

- [ ] Communication
- [ ] Connect with Corporate HR/Hiring Manager
- [ ] Share market details and sourcing metrics
- [ ] Re-define direction/pivot

At **CornerOffice**, we know that executive search is more than just a job—it's an art. With an outstanding 91% retention rate, it can transform your company's trajectory. Our talent solutions ensure you find the perfect candidates and build your teams that drive your business to new heights. **CornerOffice** delivers talent acquisition consulting services of the highest caliber. Empower your internal talent team with unbiased and independent assessments, tailored recommendations, development, and implementation.

ACKNOWLEDGEMENTS

Completing the *From Misfires to Hires* book series would not have been possible without the contributions of many individuals. Firstly, a heartfelt thank you to all the current and former members of the **CornerOffice** team. Your dedication and insights played a crucial role in shaping the concepts, systems, and processes discussed in this book.

Special recognition goes to Martha Ward for her meticulous editing, Shawna Pessillo for her thorough review, and Jodi McPhee for her design expertise. Your talents have significantly enhanced the quality of this work.

We also extend our deep gratitude to our mentors and advisors for their invaluable insights and guidance throughout our journey. To our clients, thank you for entrusting us with your recruitment needs and for providing us with the opportunities to grow and adapt in this dynamic industry.

We hope that the experiences and knowledge shared in this book will empower you, your team, and your organization to thrive in building talented teams. Thank you for allowing us to share our insights with you.

www.ingramcontent.com/pod-product-compliance
Lightning Source LLC
Chambersburg PA
CBHW071427210326
41597CB00020B/3688